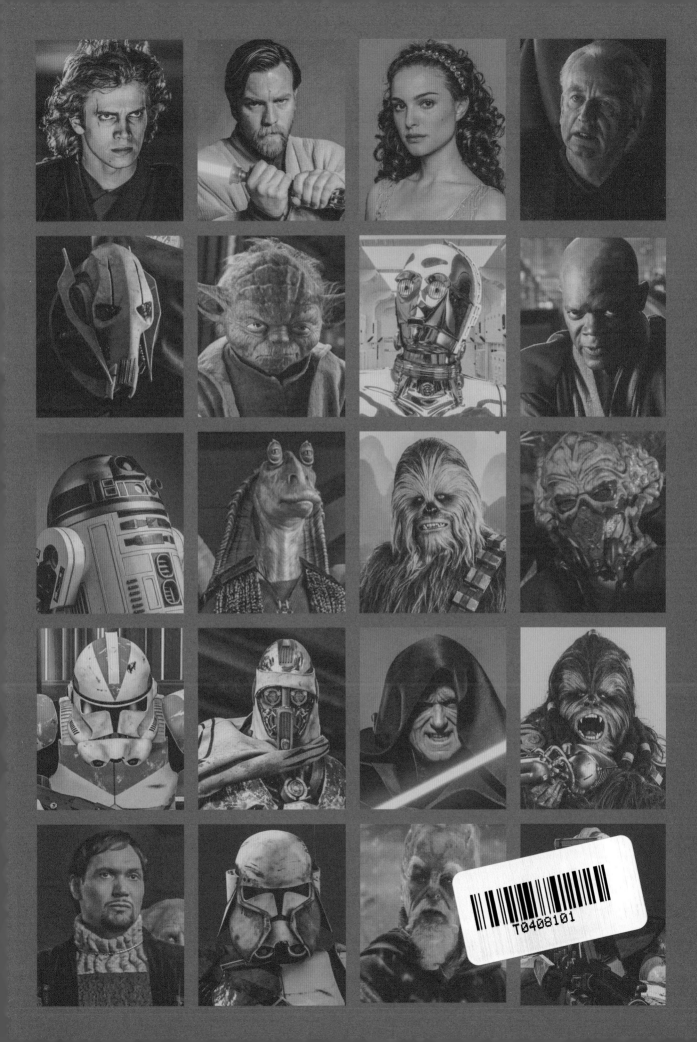

STAR WARS
REVENGE OF THE SITH

Star Wars: Revenge of the Sith was not merely the final chapter in George Lucas' prequel trilogy, it also closed the circle on a story that had taken the filmmaker more than three decades to complete.

What had begun as an idea for a *Flash Gordon*-style popcorn action-adventure movie had become a phenomenon it its own right, and the original trilogy the stuff of cinematic legend. *Star Wars: The Phantom Menace* had taken audiences back to the galaxy far, far away in 1999, and work on the final chapter of the prequel trilogy was already underway when *Star Wars: Attack of the Clones* opened in 2002. Throughout, *Star Wars Insider* continued to have unprecedented access to the people who would bring the epic conclusion of the saga to the big screen.

As with the previous two movies, producer Rick McCallum provided regular updates on the production's progress, from its conceptual stages through to the final days on set and the recording of John Williams' incredible score. Presenting exclusive interviews with the cast and crew, the long-running official magazine was in a unique position to document the making of one of the most anticipated finales of all time.

TITAN EDITORIAL
Editor Christopher Cooper
Contributors Tricia Barr, Jason Fry, Pablo Hidalgo, Frank Parisi, Amy Ratcliffe, Brett Rector, Lucas Seastrom, Jay Stobie, Chris Trevas, Daniel Wallace
Group Editor Jake Devine
Art Director Oz Browne
Editorial Assistant Holly Smith
Production Controllers Caterina Falqui & Kelly Fenton
Production Manager Jackie Flook
Sales & Circulation Manager Steve Tothill
Marketing Coordinator Lauren Noding
Direct Market Sales Coordinator Chief Stride
Publicity Manager Will O'Mullane
Publicist Caitlin Storer
Digital & Marketing Manager Jo Teather

Head of Creative & Business Development Duncan Baizley
Publishing Directors Ricky Claydon & John Dziewiatkowski
Chief Operating Officer Andrew Sumner
Publishers Vivian Cheung & Nick Landau

Star Wars: Revenge of the Sith 20th Anniversary Special Edition is published by Titan Magazines, a division of Titan Publishing Group Limited, 144 Southwark Street, London SE1 0UP

First Edition June 2025
Printed in China

For sale in the U.S., Canada, U.K., and Eire
ISBN: 9781787746725
Titan Authorized User. TCN 4883

No part of this publication may be reproduced, stored in a retrieval system, or transmitted, in any form or by any means, without the prior written permission of the publisher.

A CIP catalogue record for this title is available from the British Library.
10 9 8 7 6 5 4 3 2 1

DISTRIBUTION
U.S. Distribution:
Penguin Random House
U.K. Distribution:
MacMillan Distribution
Direct Sales Market:
Diamond Comic Distributors
General Inquiries:
customerservice@titanpublishingusa.com

eucomply OÜ Pärnu mnt 139b-14 11317
Tallinn, Estonia
hello@eucompliancepartner.com
+3375690241.

LUCASFILM EDITORIAL
Senior Editor Brett Rector
Creative Director Michael Siglain
Art Director Troy Alders
Story Group Leland Chee, Pablo Hidalgo, Kate Izquierdo
Creative Art Manager Phil Szostak
Asset Management Shahana Alam, Chris Argyropoulos, Allison Bird, Jackey Cabrera, Elinor De La Torre, Gabrielle Levenson, Nick Miano, Bryce Pinkos, Sarah Williams.

Special Thanks:
Ryan Jalernpan & Kevin Pearl

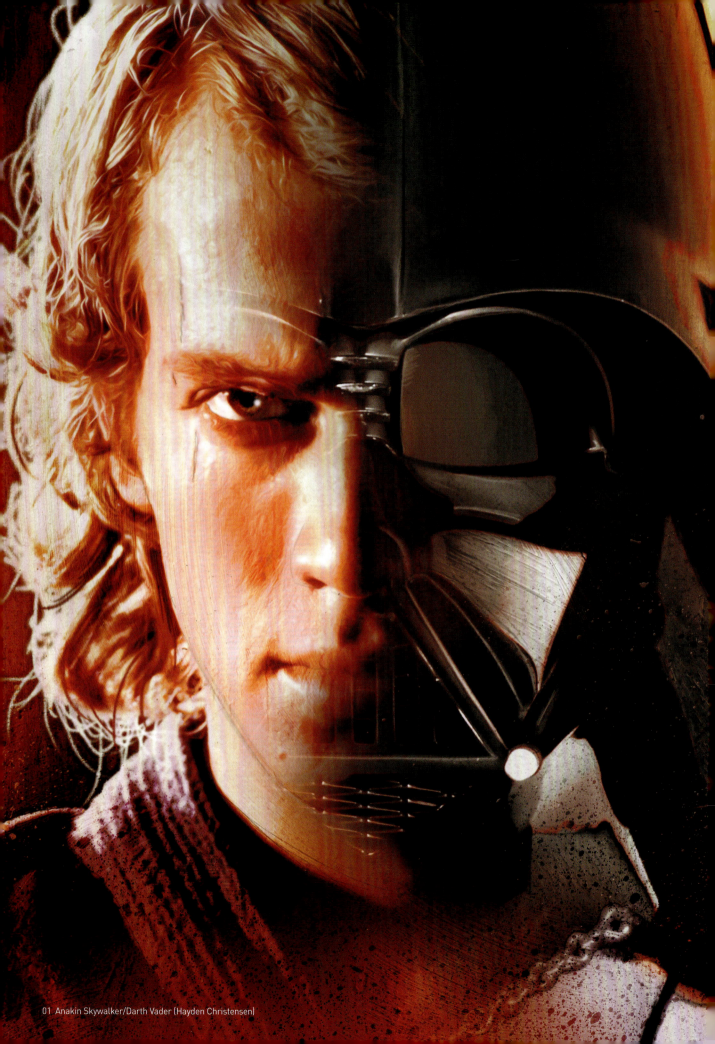

01 Anakin Skywalker/Darth Vader (Hayden Christensen)

STAR WARS: REVENGE OF THE SITH SPECIAL

CONTENTS

04	Balance of the Force
06	The Power of Love
14	The End of the Beginning
24	Fallen Jedi: Hayden Christensen
28	Torn Apart: Natalie Portman
32	Blue Sky Thinking: Concept Art
40	The High Ground: Ewan McGregor
44	Keeping the Peace: Samuel L. Jackson
48	Material Worlds: Costumes
54	Creating Kashyyyk
62	Unlimited Power: Ian McDiarmid
66	Voice of Evil: Matthew Wood
70	Order 66: The Hammer Falls
78	A Musical Journey: John Williams
84	Sith Unseen: Beyond the Movie
92	The Saga Continues

STAR WARS: REVENGE OF THE SITH SPECIAL

FALL OF THE JEDI

BALANCE OF THE FORCE

The final shot on the slate for *Star Wars: Revenge of the Sith* was completed at Fox Studios in Sydney, Australia, in the early evening of September 17, 2003. With a mountain of visual effects, audio recording, editing, and additional filming still to be done, work on the movie was far from over, but as per tradition, the final shot of principal photography would be marked with a speech from the director to all those lucky enough to have been on set that day.

"I must say this is actually the funnest film I've ever worked on," director George Lucas told the assembled crew members. "It's been very easy, and it's been very swift. It happens because everybody works in harmony, which is really important." He continued by adding, "I think we made a great movie. I'm really looking forward to cutting it together and seeing what happens."

Such sentiments were a long way from Lucas' experiences when making *Star Wars: A New Hope*, several decades earlier. Back then, he had faced disinterest from studio executives who thought the movie would be an expensive flop, and disbelief from an English crew who thought he was crazy. When the box office said otherwise, the success of the first movie allowed Lucas to become independent of the Hollywood system and make his movies just the way he wanted to. Not only that, but he was able to finance innovations in movie-making technology that would revolutionize the entire industry, to the point where he could make a new series of *Star Wars* films that matched his imagination.

In addition, when Lucas returned to make the prequel trilogy, he could call upon the talents of a new generation of creative people to support him in his endeavors; people who had a deep understanding and respect for the galaxy he had created as many of them had sought a career in the industry because of *Star Wars*.

By the very nature of its tale of betrayal and loss, *Revenge of the Sith* was destined to be the darkest of the series, but it would also be among the most memorable, bringing the epic space opera to a close in suitably grandiose style with a glimmer of hope at the end.

01 The final image of *Star Wars: Revenge of the Sith* served as a reminder to audiences that hope was on the horizon.

4 | STAR WARS: REVENGE OF THE SITH

REVENGE OF THE SITH
By Numbers

1 Kitchen sink hidden as debris in the opening space battle

5 Senate pods thrown at Yoda (and 1 thrown back at Palpatine)

47 Practical models built and shot by Industrial Light & Magic

140 minutes Running time

1,083 Effects shots involving animation

375,040 Individual frames delivered by ILM

$108,435,841 Opening weekend box office gross

$850,035,635 Worldwide Box Office Gross

Key Dates

First day of principal photography: June 30, 2003
Final day of principal photography: September 17, 2003
Teaser Trailer released: November 05, 2004
Full Trailer released: March 10, 2005
Novelization published: April 02, 2005
U.S. premiere: May 13, 2005
Home Video release: November 01, 2005

THE POWER OF LOVE

Why does Anakin Skywalker's need to recreate the parental connection he lost as a child overshadow the bonds created by love in his adult life? And if absolute power corrupts absolutely, how dangerous can the power of love become?

Fans who attended the centerpiece *Star Wars: Revenge of the Sith* panel at 2005's *Star Wars* Celebration III convention in Indianapolis had the treat of watching the opening scene of the movie a month before its release. After screening the high-octane footage, where Obi-Wan Kenobi and Anakin Skywalker ran the gauntlet in their Jedi starfighters, host Rick McCallum, the movie's executive producer, asked the audience if they wanted to hear him talk about the movie or watch the scene again. The audience chose wisely: a second viewing. With the booming pulse of war drums and a sweeping shot that follows the starfighters through the massive space battle over Coruscant, the movie establishes that the Clone War—which began in the Outer Rim at the conclusion of *Star Wars: Attack of the Clones* (2002)—had reached the very heart of the galaxy.

Politics of War

Episode III is the culmination of visionary George Lucas' prequel trilogy, and like all his work was influenced by the real-life events that shaped his worldview. Born in 1944, Lucas grew up in an era that was heavily impacted by World War II, and the iconography of this global conflict is pervasive throughout *Star Wars*. In the original trilogy, the Empire overtly evokes the Nazi fascist dictatorship, for example. The parable of Episodes I through III more broadly, however, reflect the political climate of the 1990s, the time period when the story of Anakin Skywalker's fall was germinating in Lucas' mind.

The concluding years of the Cold War in the late 80s mirrored the events of the original trilogy: evil dictators and oppressive regimes fell, ushering in a new era of optimism for democracy across Eastern Europe. Yet despite the success of America's philosophical arm wrestling with the Soviet Union, Lucas' generation had grown up in a time of huge domestic social upheaval. They still harbored suspicions of the U.S. government, which had raised a banner for equality and justice elsewhere but resisted the claims of civil rights and anti-war protestors within its own borders.

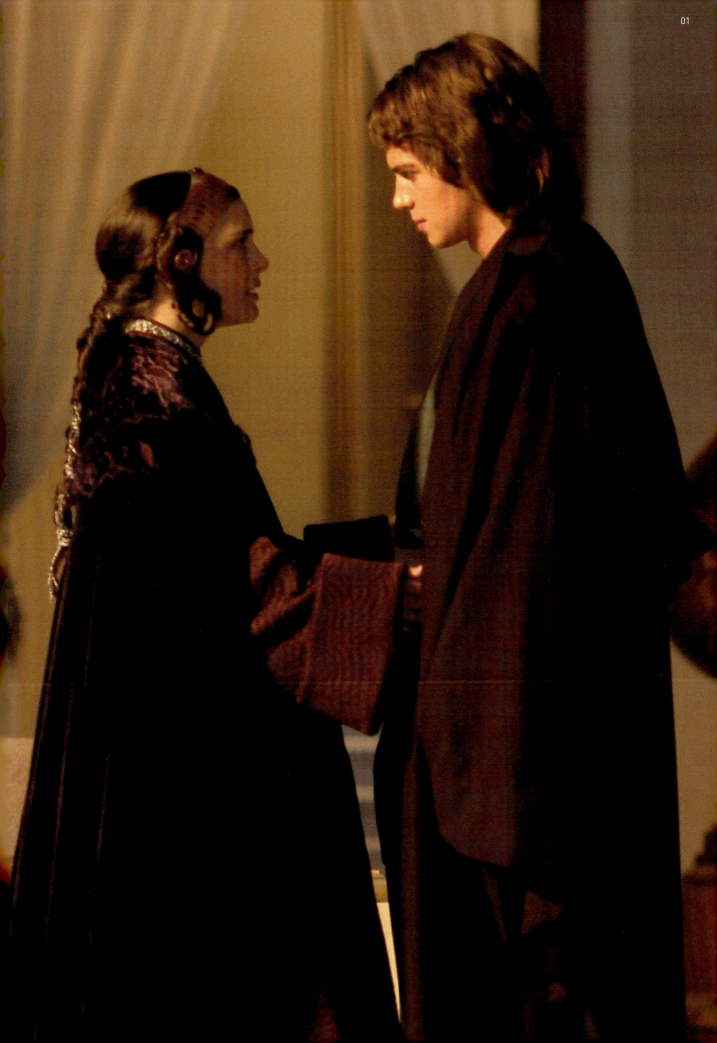

STAR WARS: REVENGE OF THE SITH SPECIAL
THE POWER OF LOVE

02

01 Previous page: Padmé Amidala (Natalie Portman) and Anakin Skywalker (Hayden Christensen) share a rare moment alone.

02 The battle for the galaxy reached Coruscant in the film's opening act.

03 Obi-Wan Kenobi's (Ewan McGregor) Jedi starfighter is attacked by buzz droids.

04 Anakin swoops in to assist his master.

05 Supreme Chancellor Palpatine (Ian McDiarmid), Obi-Wan Kenobi (McGregor) and Anakin Skywalker (Christensen) captured by General Grievous.

In the absence of the U.S.-Russian stalemate, political uncertainty opened the door for smaller despots to make power grabs, such as Iraqi leader Saddam Hussein, whose invasion of Kuwait in 1990 threatened America's interests, particularly in oil. President George H.W. Bush rallied a worldwide coalition of forces to drive Hussein out of Kuwait. While some viewed the military operation as a necessity, others believed the enormous military industrial complex (which had grown during the Cold War) was influencing political motivations for their own profit.

This distrust in the industry of war plays out on an epic scale in *Revenge of the Sith*. The Republic's adversary is named a Confederacy of Independent Systems, but their actions are controlled by a conglomeration of corporate entities: the Trade Federation, the InterGalactic Banking Clan, the Techno Union, the Retail Caucus, the Commerce Guild, and the Corporate Alliance.

Japan's attack at Pearl Harbor rallied the U.S. into World War II, even though the Hawaiian Islands are more than 2,000 miles from the continental United States. The 1990s saw a series of major terrorist attacks on U.S. soil, including the World Trade Center in New York City (1993), the federal building in Oklahoma City (1995), the Olympics in Atlanta (1996), and—as Lucas was completing Episode II—the September 11 attacks in 2001. Public agencies used these incidents to rapidly expand methods to surveil and track suspected terrorists, sparking a public outcry against invasions of civil liberties and politicians overstepping their mandated boundaries that continues to this day.

With the Whitewater scandal and Monica Lewinsky affair, President Bill Clinton's behavior brought a new level of distrust of people in power as Congress became bogged down in impeachment proceedings.

STAR WARS: REVENGE OF THE SITH SPECIAL
THE POWER OF LOVE

His successor, George W. Bush, pivoted the retaliatory anti-terrorist military action in Afghanistan in 2002 into a second invasion of Iraq in early 2003, projecting the U.S. into a much broader role in the region than originally contemplated. Although the Separatists are the Republic's battlefield opponent in *Revenge of the Sith*, the movie pulls back the curtain on the enemy within: Darth Sidious. The Sith Lord, in his role as Sheev Palpatine, uses corruption within the democratic system to rise to the position of Chancellor and then exploits the war, political machinations, and corporate greed to gradually consolidate power.

STAR WARS: REVENGE OF THE SITH SPECIAL
THE POWER OF LOVE

A Father Figure

As the movie opens, the Separatist Fleet has breached the Core and their leader, General Grievous, holds Chancellor Palpatine captive on his flagship, where Skywalker and Kenobi race to save him. Although Anakin sometimes calls Obi-Wan a father figure, the Jedi Master acknowledges after their fateful duel that they were brothers. This parallels iconic mythic struggles between siblings from Cain and Abel in the Bible and Quran to William Shakespeare's *Hamlet*, and in modern times from John Steinbeck's *East of Eden* to classic TV series *Dallas'* Bobby and J.R. Ewing.

But it's not Kenobi who has become the steadfast confidant and trusted ear of Skywalker; the avuncular Palpatine is the parental figure who accepts the brooding young man for who he is, rather than trying to change him into who the Jedi think he should be. In *Star Wars: The Phantom Menace* (1999), Anakin's mother played a crucial role in Skywalker being a happy and good person despite his circumstances. Shmi wants a better life for her son and offers him reassurance as he walks out of her life and embarks on a new, hopeful adventure. Deep down in Anakin's psyche exists the little boy whose mother told him to never look back and sent him on his way with a promise of a better future. As an adult, Anakin still craves that trusted guiding hand.

After Kenobi is knocked unconscious in their duel with Count Dooku, Skywalker bests the Sith master, dismembering both his hands. Encouraged by the captive Palpatine, Skywalker decapitates Dooku, then immediately regrets it because it's not the Jedi way. Amid his persuasive reassurance that Dooku was "too dangerous to be kept alive," the Chancellor reveals to the audience that Skywalker had confided in him about the slaughter of the Tusken Raiders after his mother's death. It is from this non-judgmental position of a surrogate father figure that Sidious suggests to his future apprentice that sometimes revenge is acceptable.

In this moment, Skywalker is embarking on a new adventure; it is not as stark as the scene where Shmi bids him farewell, but the Jedi Knight's descent into moral decline, and ultimately to becoming a Sith Lord, has begun. As much as his love for Padmé Amidala blinds Skywalker, so too does his desire for a parental figure obscure his ability to recognize Palpatine's true intentions.

Compounding the manipulation, Palpatine offers Skywalker truths throughout the movie. The Jedi are afraid of Anakin's power. The Council is planning to betray him.

06

07

08

09

STAR WARS: REVENGE OF THE SITH SPECIAL
THE POWER OF LOVE

06 Since their first meeting on Naboo, Palpatine (McDiarmid) had kept a close eye on Anakin.

07 Anakin (Christensen) found a father figure and trusted friend in Palpatine.

08 At the behest of Palpatine, Skywalker mercilessly struck down Count Dooku, despite knowing it was an act unbecoming a Jedi.

09 When Anakin learned that his mentor was a Sith Lord, he was conflicted and unsure what to do.

During a key scene when they are attending the opera, Palpatine insidiously preys upon Skywalker's greatest fear: that he could lose the person he loves and the Jedi will do nothing to stop it. While the movie doesn't explicitly say Palpatine knows about Anakin's secret marriage to Padmé, the implication is that this too is something confided between the pair. As Palpatine plants the notion that the Jedi and Sith aren't so different in Anakin's mind, he offers the seeds of hope that there is a power to keep loved ones from dying. This isn't a power that a Jedi would seek; their code forbids attachments, after all. In this moment, Anakin Skywalker's bridge to becoming Darth Vader has been built. Now all the young Jedi must do is walk across it, just like he did years ago when he took those fateful steps away from his mother.

STAR WARS: REVENGE OF THE SITH SPECIAL

THE POWER OF LOVE

10 Obi-Wan (McGregor) and Anakin (Christensen) became like brothers during the conflict of the Clone Wars.

11 Anakin's love for Padmé (Portman) paradoxically resulted in her tragic demise.

12 Following his battle with Kenobi, Anakin (Christensen), now Darth Vader, became more machine than man as the Emperor's medical droids reconstruct his severely damaged body.

Brothers at War

The bonds forged by men who fight side-by-side in wars are central to Hollywood's rise to prominence in storytelling after the close of World War II. *Revenge of the Sith* plays to the audience's cinematic and mythic understanding of how war forges fraternal bonds where they haven't existed previously. In the tragedy of Anakin Skywalker and Obi-Wan Kenobi, we observe the sundering of a brotherhood between two men, built on a decade of conjoined service as Jedi Knights and strengthened over the course of long years of war.

Episode III begins as that war ends, the two Jedi swooping through the chaos of a full-scale invasion in their starfighters. Visually, Skywalker, in his yellow starfighter, is set apart from Kenobi in his maroon starfighter, which matches the color of the rest of the Republic fleet. Yellow is ripe with conflicting meaning. It can represent optimism, energy, and loyalty, but it is sometimes associated with cowardice and deceit, all of which Skywalker embodies over the course of the movie.

The film's beginning showcases why the Jedi duo have become standouts in the war. They are bold and fearsome fighters, slipping through a minimal opening onto Grievous' flagship and dispatching droid troops in the hanger with relative ease. The scene ends with them in a back-to-back pose that will later be echoed by Rey and Kylo Ren in *Star Wars: The Last Jedi*'s (2017) throne room battle.

Throughout this opening act, Kenobi and Skywalker's bond is brought to the fore: during the space battle, Anakin wants to go back and help his clone wingmen, but heeds Obi-Wan's command to stay on mission; fearing his fighter is lost to buzz droids, Kenobi implores his apprentice to press on alone, but Skywalker refuses to let his master perish in space. His first attempt at saving his master is both rash and unhelpful, but once it is apparent Skywalker isn't going to give up on his friend, Kenobi doesn't try to press him on the matter, signaling that he is aware of his Padawan's emotional limitations as a Jedi.

Revenge of the Sith perfectly threads the needle in Obi-Wan Kenobi's characterization, balancing his portrayal as a heroic yet flawed man, one who often sees the moral quagmire he is standing in but can't quite overcome decades of ingrained Jedi dogma. He rightfully doesn't trust Palpatine, but is also troubled with tasking his apprentice to spy on a person he knows he admires. Even the way Kenobi asks Padmé about the paternity of her unborn twins, a rhetorical question, suggests that he has understood the complex duality of his brother-in-arms. Yet his love for Skywalker prevents him from accepting the true extent of the deeds of which he is capable— until the holovid of his former Padawan killing younglings makes it undeniable. Most of us can relate to knowing something troubling about a person close to us, but overlooking it for the sake of love or friendship.

STAR WARS: REVENGE OF THE SITH SPECIAL

THE POWER OF LOVE

A Love Lost

That same dynamic, too, underlies the tragic love story of Anakin and Padmé. If not for the prospect of death and war, their love might have simmered and remained unrequited. War leads to tragic endings for many romances, not just those at the centerpiece of an epic monomyth.

The Skywalker-Kenobi brotherhood is at the heart of the movie's laser-sharp focus on the story surrounding Anakin's fall to the dark side, pushing the Padmé relationship into a secondary role. Perhaps her death was deemed inevitable in the eyes of George Lucas, with all roads leading to the showdown on the volcanic world as foretold in the original trilogy. Several deleted scenes flesh out Senator Amidala's participation in seeking a diplomatic solution to civil war, but were omitted in trying to preserve the core story of Skywalker's fall, which is motivated by fear of her demise, not her politics.

Amidala is more a plot device than an agent of her own destiny, tragic or otherwise. One beautiful moment permits the character some room to breathe though, accompanied by John Williams' heart-wrenching piece entitled 'Padmé's Ruminations.' Nothing is said, but her hopes, dreams, and worries are expressed through her eyes, juxtaposed against Skywalker's expression, displaying the fears of a young man pained by his many losses.

In that intense scene, Skywalker chooses selfishly and rushes to stop Master Mace Windu from killing his father figure, Palpatine, despite knowing that the man is a Sith Lord intent on destroying the Republic that his wife and Kenobi hold so dear. That allegiance costs Skywalker everything: his family, his best friend, his body, and his soul. He ends the movie isolated from the galaxy inside a life-sustained armored suit, with his new master and the dark side of the Force his only companions.

STAR WARS: REVENGE OF THE SITH SPECIAL

THE END OF THE BEGINNING

THE END OF THE BEGINNING

When *Star Wars* burst into the public consciousness in 1977, *A New Hope* was a one-off with no guarantee that there might be a sequel, let alone an entire trilogy of movies. Almost three decades later, *Star Wars: Revenge of the Sith* was the final chapter in a second trilogy, finally revealing how Anakin Skywalker transformed into the hate-fueled monster Darth Vader. *Star Wars Insider* followed its production from concept to screen.

"We're in total 'go' mode," *Star Wars: Revenge of the Sith* producer Rick McCallum told *Star Wars Insider* in his October 2002 prequel update. "I travel to Australia in a few weeks and close the deal for the studio. Then we go to London, and we start pulling together our entire wardrobe department. In November, we move to Australia, begin construction, and start setting up the film. We start shooting in June of next year."

By this point, a team of concept artists led by Episode II veterans Erik Tiemens and Ryan Church had already produced plenty of new ideas, having consulted with director George Lucas within a few weeks of *Attack of the Clones* arriving in theaters. McCallum was keen to emphasize that everything remained in the concept stage. "We're working on broad strokes of things rather than anything specific."

The reason for this was that Lucas was yet to complete the script for the movie. "He's just started writing," confirmed McCallum. "I can't go very far without him. But I'm trying to put as much pressure on George as possible. Guilt is the only leverage you ever have with a writer," he joked.

"This conceptual stage is really to help George start to imagine the world," the producer continued. "Here's the way it works. George won't say, 'Oh, I want this bottle, and it's got a blue label.' He says, 'There should be something—and I don't know what it is—but we should design something we can drink out of.' And then we get ten different ideas, and he takes the bottle cap from one, the label from another, the shape from a third. That's just the process with him, and it's enough to generate some cool designs. George's talent is his ability to cut and paste. It's evolutionary. It's in relation to what he's seeing, what he's thinking at that moment, where he thinks the story should go. It's a remarkable process to watch as it unfolds.

"On one level, he's the supreme collage artist, because that's what all film editors do. That's what he loves doing more than anything else. Taking this line of dialogue and putting it over there and changing the story. That's what pure filmmaking is about."

Beyond the creative process, McCallum had already begun work on managing the production, which would embrace new technology. "We're trying to push the nature of digital technology in creating digital sets because it's much more cost efficient and allows us much more freedom. That takes a long time. We're starting to look at the editorial department. I've got to lock in all the logistics of where we're shooting in each country. I've got to scout locations and set the basic commitments that I'm going to make in Australia, Spain, Italy, England, and wherever else it is that we end up shooting. I have to hire the construction crew, which numbers around 400 people, to be ready to start building sets in November. There's a lot of stuff that's happening. Luckily, I have a great team of people that I worship and adore, and we've all been together for a long time."

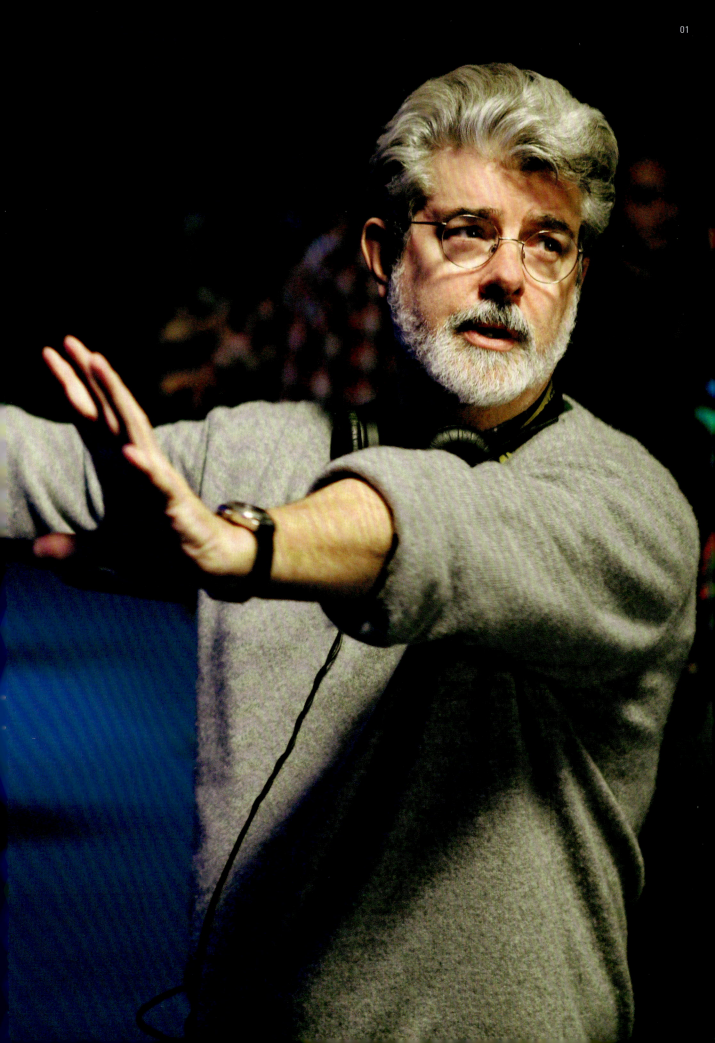

STAR WARS: REVENGE OF THE SITH SPECIAL
THE END OF THE BEGINNING

01 Previous page: Director George Lucas.

02 John Knoll (left) and George Lucas (center) preparing to shoot a pyrotechnic explosion on Obi-Wan Kenobi's Jedi starfighter.

03 Knoll and Lucas discuss the framing of the shot.

04 (Left to right) Ian McDiarmid (Supreme Chancellor Palpatine), Hayden Christensen (Anakin Skywalker) and Ewan McGregor (Obi-Wan Kenobi) shoot a stunt sequence against a blue screen. In post, it would become the interior of General Grievous' ship.

As preparations gathered pace, McCallum was quick to shoot down online buzz regarding potential filming locations as 2002 came to a close. "Never believe rumors you read on the internet," he sagely advised. In fact, he was yet to begin location scouting, waiting for production designer Gavin Bocquet to join the film.

"Gavin's job is to make everything that Erik Tiemens and Ryan Church work on in the conceptual stage become reality. Remember, everything in the *Star Wars* world has to be designed. Once you have the look of the planet, you have to create its own culture, its technology, its costumes, its vehicles, what the props look like, what kinds of houses people live in. When you have a lot of planets, that's a very serious amount of work."

Although still awaiting a finished script, he did let slip a few hints as to how the saga would resolve itself. "I can't promise a happy ending," he admitted. Yet McCallum wasn't concerned about a potentially downbeat finale. "I think we'll be given a lot more leeway there because most people understand that this is just a chapter. Yes, the film has to work within its own context and work as a film complete unto itself, but when we're talking about the issues that we have to deal with, there's not a lot of light there. Most people who know the *Star Wars* saga know that this is Anakin's destiny."

The costume department, headed by designer Trisha Biggar, began their work in mid-November. "It's a big deal," McCallum told *Insider* in his December update. "We'll probably make another twelve hundred costumes, so it's a big operation. George has approved about ten of them."

The bulk of those costumes would be worn by background artists and extras. "We'll limit the search for people who are 5 foot 7 inches or 5 foot 10 inches, or who can fit into a [specific] costume," McCallum explained. "We cast every single extra, so it's not like a cattle call where we call up an agency and say we want 30 people. We are more interested in the overall look than the specific person."

In January 2003, the production art department had moved to Sydney, while the concept artists at Skywalker Ranch—now joined by Sang Jun Lee, working alongside Iain

STAR WARS: REVENGE OF THE SITH SPECIAL

THE END OF THE BEGINNING

McCaig on costume concepts—had produced more than fifteen hundred illustrations. McCallum had also headed Down Under to oversee the gargantuan task of preparing Fox Studios in Sydney for filming. "It's like moving a small army in," he said.

While economic reasons had been part of the reason for principal photography on the *Star Wars* prequels to move from London to Australia, the filmmakers had found their new home to be especially suitable for their needs.

"It's not laid out like a traditional studio," explained McCallum. "It used to be an old fairground. It's got a really great atmosphere, the people who run the studio are terrific. It's very open. It's got parkland. There's a cricket stadium right next to it. There are wonderful shops and theaters adjacent to it. It's a really nice, easy, wonderful place to make a movie. I love England. I love English crews. But it's very, very expensive now in terms of hotels, apartments, dinner, and transportation. It's not as easy. Australia is, without question, the easiest and most cost-effective place to shoot in the English language, anywhere in the world."

While McCallum was busy getting infrastructure in place, Gavin Bocquet was headed to San Francisco. "He's got a whole bunch of models that we went through just before Christmas that he's going to show George," McCallum relayed. "Hopefully George will approve those, and then we'll have the first two or three small sets that we can start building by the end of next week."

Meanwhile, the lead cast were wrapping up film projects and preparing for their return to the *Star Wars* galaxy. "Ewan McGregor is shooting a Tim Burton picturing in Georgia," McCallum reported. "Natalie Portman just finished *Cold Mountain*, which is being shot in Romania." As for Hayden Christensen? "I know he's working out like mad. He's beefing up," the producer confirmed. "Hayden wants to come over about four or five weeks before filming, because he's got a lot of things to work on with stunt coordinator Nick Gillard on all the fight sequences. Same with Ewan. And then Natalie will have a lot of costume fittings, so she'll have to come in for them."

05 The clapperboard for *Star Wars* Episode III.

06 Anthony Daniels (C-3PO) recording temporary dialogue tracks in an edit suite.

STAR WARS: REVENGE OF THE SITH | 17

STAR WARS: REVENGE OF THE SITH SPECIAL

THE END OF THE BEGINNING

Come March, and McCallum reported that although the film's screenplay was yet to be completed, Lucas had delivered an outline and forty-six pages of script. The producer wasn't overly concerned, however. "We only got a script two days before we started Episode II," he recalled. Asked how much of the current draft was likely to change, he joked, "All of it!" adding, "In terms of costumes and sets, we know what we're doing, but in terms of the actual dialogue and some key action sequences, that'll change all the way up until the day the film is released. It's like building a house when you don't have all the plans."

With cameras set to start rolling in June, the preceding months were filled with video conferences between department heads in Sydney and Lucas at the Skywalker Ranch. "We e-mail all the perspective drawings and models to George, and we go through them usually Mondays, Wednesdays, and Fridays," said McCallum. "Teams are doing well. Set construction's been going on for about 3 weeks. We do sections of sets because we don't have all our stages yet. Each set we complete on the stage itself." At this point, Lucas had approved fifty-two sets, including "lots of vehicles."

Months before principal photography commenced, the pre-visualization team began choreographing the movie. "They've been working for about six weeks," reported McCallum. "And we have Ben Burtt editing the animatics, so that's going along great."

The pre-vis team had already produced about three minutes of animation for the earliest scenes of the movie and paved the way for work to come. "When you start, you've got to build so many models," explained McCallum. "There's a lot of work that has to be done. In about a month's time, we'll be able to pump out fifty to sixty shots a week."

Five days before principal photography began, McCallum reported feeling, "A great sense of dread," at the imminent arrival of George Lucas, "Because George equals changes!"

Sure enough, Lucas had made several key alterations since his first draft script. "It's a pretty dramatic change," said McCallum, noting that he expected the fourth draft to be finished the following day (June 25). With internet rumors rife regarding the title of the new movie, the producer said fans would have to continue calling it by its episode number for a while yet, as Lucas had yet to reveal the title even to his producer. "He's got a title," McCallum confided, "but when he'll tell us could be months away."

The director wasted little time after arriving in Sydney. "[George] has got a very tight schedule," confirmed McCallum. "He starts about 6:30 a.m. and spends a couple of hours on the script. Then he does a shot walkthrough for about an hour and a half with [director of photography] David Tattersall. We usually shoot tests for half an hour: Hair, makeup, and lighting tests on the set. Then he spends about an hour and a half with the stunt coordinator. He rehearses with the actors from 2 p.m. until five, then we go over any changes he's made that day, working through the schedule, and making adjustments on each day's shooting. And then it's home, dinner, and start all over again."

Lucas was the last of the major players to reach Sydney, following the arrival of Natalie Portman a few weeks prior. All three principal cast members had full schedules, every day. When not rehearsing, McCallum reported, "they're either in wardrobe fittings, makeup tests, or working out."

Ewan McGregor and Hayden Christensen had fight training incorporated into their busy calendars. While Christensen already had a few weeks' head start in physical training and choreography, McGregor wasn't far behind as Nick Gillard had visited him on set in Alabama while the actor had still been engaged on his Tim Burton project. "So, even though he wasn't with us, he was still training," the producer explained.

Over on the soundstages, the initial sets were almost ready. "The first wave of five is complete," updated McCallum. "We just had our walkthrough of Padmé's apartment, and that's all been approved for set dressing, painting, and everything else."

As soon as shooting was completed on one set, the crew would tear it down and build another. "We usually have seven stages and about ten sets on those seven stages," explained McCallum. "We have sixty-two sets, so we have five major turnovers throughout the approximately sixty days of shooting." To populate those sets, a group of three hundred extras had been assembled, fewer than a third as many as for the previous film. "This is a much more intimate story," revealed McCallum.

07 Ewan McGregor, Hayden Christensen, and Count Dooku stunt double Kyle Rowling filming a lightsaber duel on the *Invisible Hand* set.

08 A remote-control R2-D2 prop, minus the droid's familiar dome.

09 Padmé Amidala's apartment set under construction at Fox Studios, Sydney.

STAR WARS: REVENGE OF THE SITH SPECIAL

THE END OF THE BEGINNING

At the midway point in the shooting schedule, the producer admitted that he felt "relieved more than excited" at the milestone. "I've been here for eleven months and I'm ready to go home," he told *Insider*. Natalie Portman had completed her scenes as Padmé and returned to the U.S., and the atmosphere on set had subtly shifted. "It changed the day Natalie left," intimated McCallum. "That side of the story has completely gone, and we don't have any major drama sequences coming now. It's just pure action."

In the event, principal photography was completed five days ahead of schedule, but the film was a long way from being completed. With pickup shots planned (to be filmed in both Sydney and London), the long process of post-production got underway.

With Thanksgiving just a fortnight away, *Insider* caught up with the producer again at Skywalker Ranch, where the challenge was to complete a rough cut of the entire movie by the holiday season, as well as a solid twenty-five-minute sequence to be handed over to Industrial Light & Magic by Janurary 5, 2004, so that visual effects work could officially begin.

"We're in a weird, scary place right now, but that's normal for this stage because we don't really have a movie yet," said McCallum.

The November schedule for the producer, Lucas, and editors Roger Barton and Ben Burtt was very structured and intense. Burtt was charged with honing the film's major space battles, fight sequences, and digital work, while Barton cut the dramatic portions of the film. Both met with Lucas daily "to go straight through the movie, actually assembling the picture and creating the first rough cut of Episode III," according to McCallum. At that point, they were already about halfway through the process, which would continue into Spring 2004.

"Editors piece a movie together shot by shot," explained Burtt, who was working on a scene featuring Obi-Wan Kenobi when *Insider* met with him at Skywalker Ranch. "In a way, what we do is like writing. The director provides the 'words,' and the editor builds the 'sentences,' which are the scenes. Put together, they tell a story."

On one of the four computer monitors at Burtt's workstation was an image of actor McGregor paused mid-jump in front of a greenscreen. Burtt was preparing to add elements to this shot, which needed to be sent on to the animatics team.

"We work with at least eight layers of video elements," he explained. "Backgrounds, middle grounds, foregrounds—anything that is important for telling the story. Everything in this room is done in a 'collage state.' We adapt previsualized scenes and then add every other element that's going to be in there—characters, flying spaceships, beams of light—then we send it to animatics, and they make it look much better."

The director would regularly catch up with other departments, including the animatics team. "When George is working with the animatics team, he's studying visual effects shots that are being animated for use as placeholders for the rough cut of the complete film that we'll view before Christmas," said McCallum. "What we'll see will be very crude, with weird background paintings and shots that won't be dynamic, but they will give us a good indication of where we're at with everything." He added, "Even though we are doing work now, building spaceship models and digital environments, and conducting research and development, the real work for ILM doesn't begin until January."

10

11

A crucial deadline for ILM was met on January 8 when the visual effects crew received the first major action sequence of Episode III, an intense and fast-paced space battle between Republic and Separatist forces. A small group of ILM staff, along with Lucas, McCallum, Burtt, Barton, visual effects supervisor John Knoll, animation director Rob Coleman, and art department supervisors Ryan Church and Erik Tiemens assembled at the Company's "C" Theatre in San Rafael to watch this twenty-minute sequence as part of the first run of "dailies" for 2004, a weekly occurrence at ILM during movie production.

The two-hour session ended with a promise from Lucas to Knoll that the first two reels of Episode III would be delivered to ILM "very soon." He also informed Knoll that fifty-two more scenes were being turned over that week to the animatics department at Skywalker Ranch.

With an assembly cut of the movie taking longer than expected ("We're three weeks behind schedule," McCallum would admit to Insider in February 2004), pickup shoots planned for the following month at Elstree Studios in London were put back until the summer. These would be just the first of three rounds of photography that would be undertaken before the film was ready for release. An additional week of shooting was also planned for November 2004, as well as three or four days penciled in for early 2005, for last-minute touches.

"I expect that we will shoot for two six-day weeks, and it will take us four to five weeks before that to prepare for it," said McCallum. "Right now, I can tell you that we've asked Hayden Christensen, Samuel L. Jackson, Ian McDiarmid, Ewan McGregor, and Christopher Lee to join us for the pickups in August."

Live-action shots and motion-capture for the Wookiee battle were also on the schedule.

McCallum emphasized that they would be filming additional material rather than reshooting existing scenes. "We will be filming all-new scenes, which we had thought about but haven't written completely," he said. "Right now, we're still in the process of cutting scenes again. This is why we have to view the first assembly, to get an idea of what we need to shoot, and where."

Meanwhile, background plate photography was also underway, undertaken by famed cinematographer and director Ron Frick. McCallum revealed that aerial shots had been taken in and around Phuket, Thailand in May, with the shoot moving to China in late June. Frick and his team would wrap up their work in Switzerland before the end of summer, capturing background plates for the idyllic planet of Alderaan.

10 ILM modelmakers during construction of the Mustafar landscape miniature.

11 Orange lights beneath the miniature added fiery heat to its lava flow.

12 Preparing the Mustafar miniature for filming.

13

In July, McCallum took a break from preparing the upcoming shoot to make a flying visit from Shepperton Studios in London to San Diego Comic-Con International, to reveal the movie's full title for the first time—*Star Wars: Revenge of the Sith.*

With almost all of the new shots required to complete the movie in the can (or more accurately, stored on tape and hard drives) the production arrived at Elstree Studios—the home of the original trilogy—on January 31, 2005, for a single, final day of additional photography. It was a full-circle moment for director George Lucas.

"We started the studio work in here the first day for Episode IV," Lucas observed, as he surveyed the dark interior of Stage 8. "I think it was the kitchen, you know, where Aunt Beru is in there cooking, and Owen comes in looking for Luke." The soundstage had also housed the X-wing fighter and *Millennium Falcon* cockpits.

Shooting for the day consisted of four scenes where additional shots were needed to patch over continuity or accommodate a change in dialogue. As far as the cast were concerned, only Hayden Christensen and Natalie Portman were required, although they didn't share a scene and both actors were shot in isolation. Portman had completed her work by 10 a.m., effectively completing her role as Padmé.

In between the setups, McCallum took advantage of a few minutes of downtime to proudly show off a new video: the full *Revenge of the Sith* trailer that would debut a few months later in March. The small crew crowded around the single plasma screen to watch the trailer play, which included several shots gathered at the Shepperton shoot in September 2004.

Soon after shooting new elements for a scene between Anakin Skywalker and Darth Sidious, the crew moved on to the final setup, which happened to be the most complicated pickup of the lot: Anakin running and dodging along the length of crumbling architecture amid the fiery chaos of Mustafar. The framing sequences were shot in both Sydney and at Shepperton, with octagonal segments of set and a trio of wooden frames representing the falling structure, while the rest was delineated with tape on the blue floor. All Christensen had to do was run the length of the set.

"It's a bit minimal, isn't it?" exclaimed production designer Gavin Bocquet, who had already moved onto other projects but spent the day on set at Elstree to witness the final shot. "I couldn't miss the last day of *Star Wars*," said the prequel veteran, who had been one of the key members of *The Young Indiana Jones Chronicles* crew to graduate to the new *Star Wars* trilogy.

A few takes with varying camera moves were shot with Christensen running at top speed, and then it was all over.

"Last shot!" Lucas pointed out with a little fanfare. After twenty-eight years, the saga was in the can. As applause spread among the small crew, McCallum glanced at his watch. "I can't think of anything else to say, but that's lunch everyone," he announced.

"Can we watch the trailer again?" asked Christensen.

13 Ewan McGregor as Obi-Wan Kenobi securing the high ground on the Mustafar set.

14 Hayden Christensen in full costume as Darth Vader.

22 | STAR WARS: REVENGE OF THE SITH

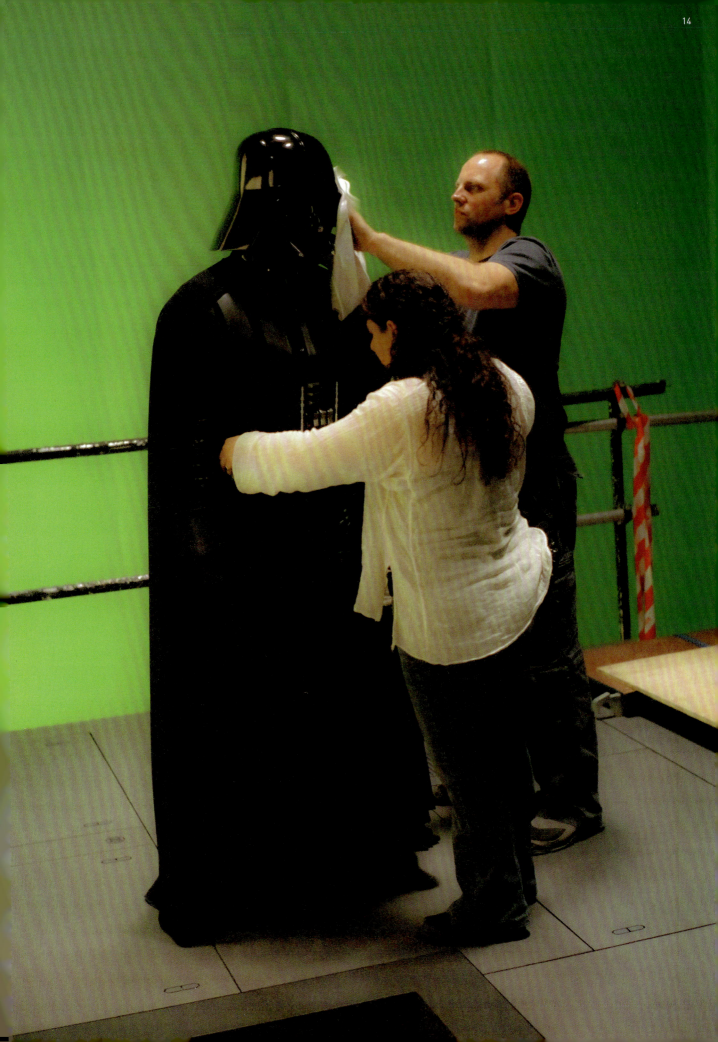

FALLEN JEDI
HAYDEN CHRISTENSEN: ANAKIN SKYWALKER

Plucked from his life as a slave on Tatooine and trained in the ways of the Force on Coruscant, Anakin Skywalker proved himself as a respected Jedi Knight during the Clone Wars. Yet the troubled young man was haunted by the inequities of his childhood; fearful that his forbidden love for Padmé Amidala would be undone; and swayed by the insidious mentorship of Supreme Chancellor Palpatine. His suffering would be the inevitable outcome.

Hayden Christensen was only 19 years old when he was cast as Anakin Skywalker in *Star Wars: Attack of the Clones*. The virtually unknown television actor faced the arduous task of not only being convincing as the young Jedi torn between duty and love, but also showing the hunger for power that would see him seduced to the dark side by the final film of the prequel trilogy. In portraying such a complex role, Christensen's task was to bridge the innocence of Jake Lloyd's Anakin in *The Phantom Menace* with the iconic villainy of Darth Vader from the original trilogy.

"It was a difficult challenge," the actor admitted in 2005 to *Star Wars Insider*. "I didn't have someone to emulate, like Ewan [McGregor] did with Alec Guinness. Yet I still had a character who was pre-defined by the other actors who had played him. It was a bit of an odd juxtaposition. Ultimately, I had to be the linear connection between the Anakin that Jake Lloyd played, and capture Darth Vader as portrayed by Sebastian Shaw when he was demasked in Return of the Jedi.

"When I'm playing a scene, I don't try to pull the experience from my own life and use them as motivation to extract a certain emotion," added Christensen. "For me, it's all about the circumstance and the situation my character is in and trying to impose whatever stimulus it is that they are reacting to, and to make that real for myself so that the performance feels right for the scene and for the progression of the character."

Despite Anakin's fall from grace, Christensen remained convinced that audiences would still feel some empathy towards the character. "You will sympathize with Anakin if you allow yourself to be seduced in the same way that Palpatine seduced him," the actor insisted. "The problem is that Anakin more or less sells his soul to the devil, and in doing so is fed a bunch of propaganda that he's forced to believe because of the position he's in. But it's all actually a con. So, you can be very sympathetic if you allow yourself to be deceived by the con as well. It's not until the last act of the film that Anakin starts to lose his cool and go outside of himself and really feeds on his ambition and the temptations that surround him."

With regards to Anakin's journey to the dark side, that progression was influenced by Supreme Chancellor Palpatine, portrayed by Ian McDiarmid, whom Christensen held in high regard.

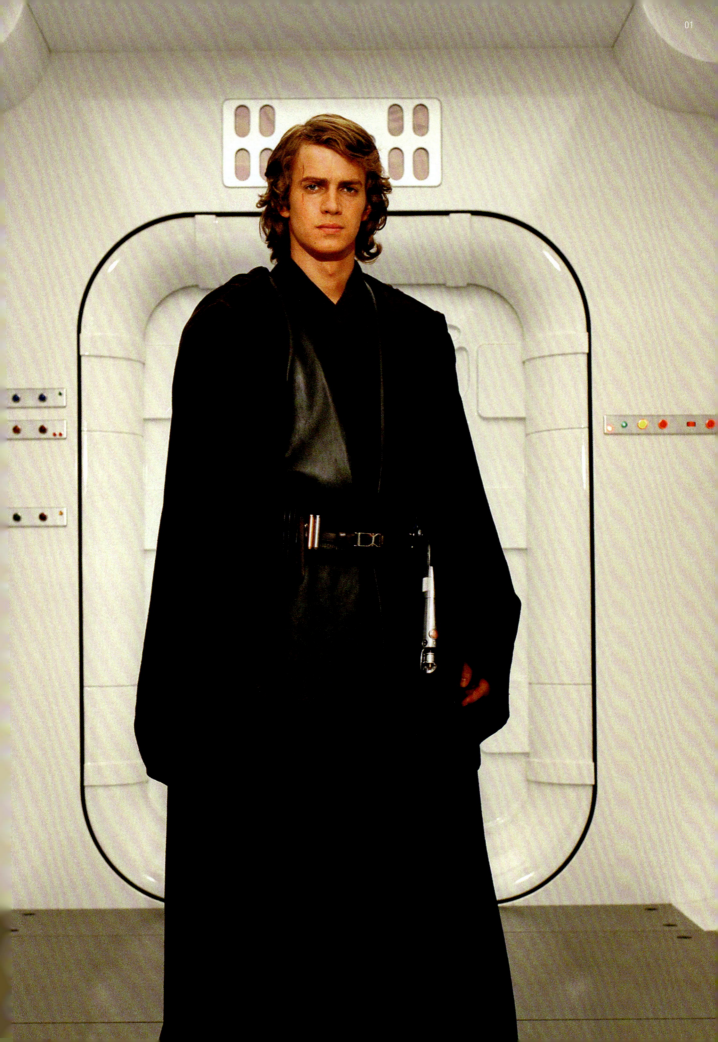

02

"He's just such a lovely man and one of the best actors I've ever had the privilege of acting with," he confirmed. "It was something I had very much looked forward to since the first table read for *Attack of the Clones*. [Ian] was always open to having a dialogue about the work and wanted to talk about the subtext of what was being played. He was always available and accessible, and he always looked like he was enjoying himself. His character is so dark and evil at times, yet he just goes in and out of it with such ease that it was amazing to watch. Working with him surpassed all my expectations. He really steals the show in the film."

The moment that everyone else had been waiting for, of course, was the return of Darth Vader. "It was thrilling," recalled Christensen, who donned the black leather suit, flowing cape, and dark helmet for the climactic transformation, with James Earl Jones returning to provide Vader's voice. "To finally get dressed up as Darth Vader felt like it gave my role some finality, some completion.

"It was really nice that they allowed me to get into the suit, because they could have just put some really tall guy in it and gotten away with it," the actor continued. "But I begged and pleaded, so they actually built a suit to fit me. They had to make a big muscle suit so that I could physically fill out the costume,

03

one of those sumo wrestling suits that you get into at a fair, which wasn't very intimidating at all!"

Conversely, for those lucky enough to be on set as the Dark Lord of the Sith made his reappearance, the atmosphere was intense. "There was a fair amount of staring when I first emerged as Darth Vader," Christensen revealed. "But for me it was more a case of trying to stay on my feet and make it up the stairs without falling over. I kept picturing how mad everyone would have been if I had tripped and scuffed the helmet or something. At the same time, when the cameras started rolling, it was quite something to stand there next to Sidious and deliver my lines. I know that my voice was replaced by James Earl Jones, but it was very empowering to speak the dialogue. It's definitely a memory I'll have for a long time."

04

26 | STAR WARS: REVENGE OF THE SITH

05

06

01 Previous page: Hayden Christensen as Anakin Skywalker.

02 Obi-Wan Kenobi (Ewan McGregor) and Anakin Skywalker arrive on General Grievous' ship.

03 Anakin and Padmé (Natalie Portman).

04 Anakin Skywalker's transformation into Darth Vader is complete.

05 Christensen during the application of his lava burn makeup.

06 A new Darth Vader costume was custom made for Christensen.

STAR WARS: REVENGE OF THE SITH | 27

TORN APART
NATALIE PORTMAN: PADMÉ AMIDALA

As the Clone Wars drew to a close, Senator Padmé Amidala found herself being pulled in two directions. On the one hand, the Republic had never been in more need of her steadfast devotion to duty; while on the other, her marriage to Jedi Anakin Skywalker wasn't the only secret she was keeping.

f all the storylines of *Revenge of the Sith*, the most tragic was the fate that befell Padmé Amidala, a woman who was as committed to her political role in the Senate as she was to her secret husband, Anakin Skywalker. Ultimately, both sides of her life would be torn apart, despite her best efforts.

"I didn't really think of them as being separate," actor Natalie Portman explained to *Star Wars Insider*. "Rather that the two sides of Padmé's life happened simultaneously, because she wouldn't have lost her man if she weren't so committed to the Republic. If she'd had a different concept of government or morality, and if her loyalties to him had been above everything else, she might have been able to stay with Anakin.

"Padmé was a pretty centered person," Portman added, "so, it wasn't like she was going through a big internal change herself. Externally, things were changing around her, and she had to make decisions to cope with that. Anakin was really the one going through change. Padmé was more reactive to what was going on with him."

Playing the part of the strong-willed senator as well as an expectant mother, did Portman see Padmé as a feminist role model?

"I definitely appreciate the fact that the role defines the true meaning of feminism as I interpret it," agreed Portman. "Feminism is often misconstrued as women wanting to be like men. True feminism, for me, is bringing out what is particular to women, because we are different. It's not about going someplace and behaving like a man, or desiring what men want just because you can get it. It is about making decisions from your point of view as to what you are going to do with the opportunities you are afforded. I think Padmé was an amazing example of that, because she was a politician and she'd been a leader of many people. But rather than being consumed with the thirst for power, as many of the people around her were, both men and women, she stayed true to her compassion and her belief in democracy, and in humanity. I think that's really important."

While Portman shared much of her screentime in *Attack of the Clones* with Hayden Christensen (Anakin Skywalker), *Revenge of the Sith* offered her the chance to play some emotional scenes with her other co-star, Ewan McGregor.

"In the first two films, the scenes we had together usually involved other people, and they didn't include anything more than a formal encounter where I played a queen or a senator and he played a Jedi, paying his respects, so it was so exciting to get to do substantive scenes with Ewan this time around," said Portman. "I respect him so much as an actor because he is serious about the work, but he is also fun to work with. He really lightens up a set. And he would do things before filming a scene that helped push me, which was very generous of him to do.

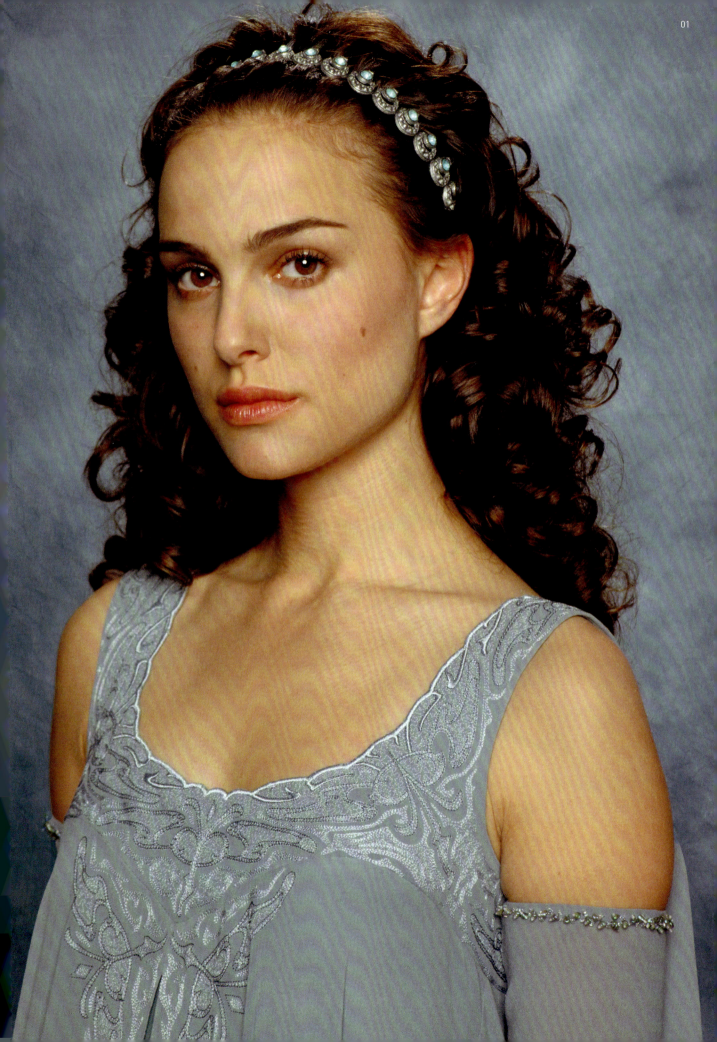

STAR WARS: REVENGE OF THE SITH SPECIAL
TORN APART

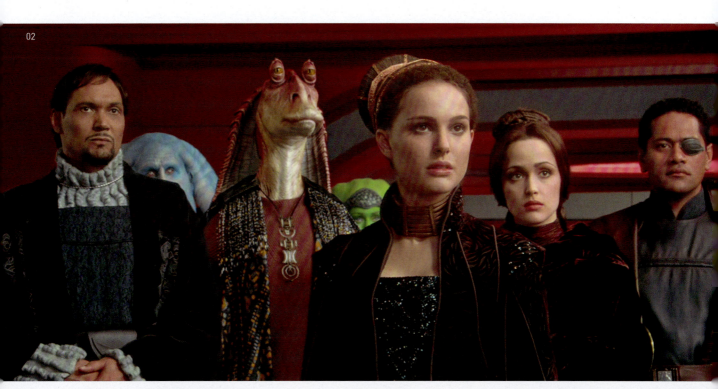

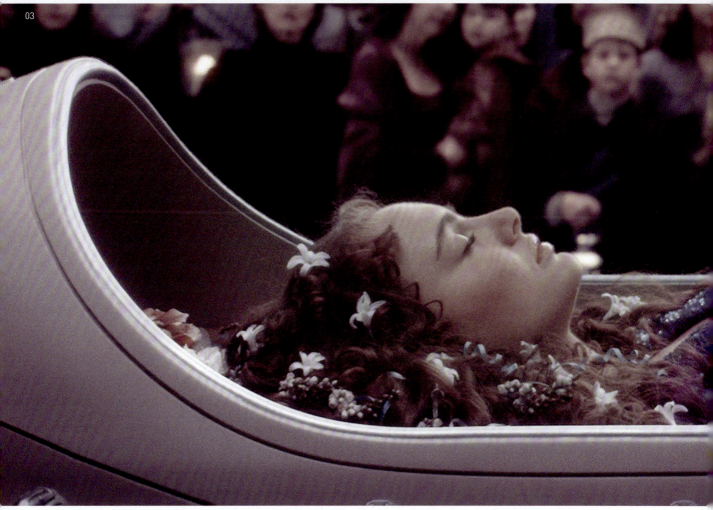

TORN APART

"The relationship between Padmé and Obi-Wan Kenobi really developed off-screen between the movies, so we went through the process of figuring out what they had been through before they got to that point," Portman continued. "Had they ever hung out alone? Were they only friends through Anakin? Did they have a separate relationship apart from that? Obi-Wan and Padmé might have become friends to the point where he felt comfortable going to her and telling her things that were very personal, dramatic, or life-changing. It was really interesting."

McGregor's supportive input also helped Portman in one of her most important scenes— Padmé's death during childbirth. Although she didn't have to reach too deep to find the right emotions.

"Just the notion of dying while giving birth to the twins was enough to get me to the point I needed to be at during that scene," the actor explained. "I really didn't have to do much other than to keep from thinking about anything else. Again, Ewan was a big help. During filming we had animatronic babies, and Ewan did the scene, talking and being very serious, while moving the puppet baby with his hands. He's the Frank Oz of the new millennium. It was pretty amazing."

Looking back over the experience of making the prequel movies, what was Portman's lasting impression?

"Because we shot the first movie in England and the final two in Australia, it felt like a new movie each time," she said. "Except this one was very well documented. Everyone was aware that each set was sort of historical, so there were crews capturing every moment, such as Anthony Daniels getting into his C-3PO costume. That's when you realize that this thing has become a cultural icon."

01 Previous page: Natalie Portman as Padmé Amidala.

02 Amidala "stayed true to her compassion and belief in democracy," said Portman.

03 Padmé Amidala's funeral on Naboo.

04 Doomed lovers Anakin Skywalker (Hayden Christensen) and Padmé Amidala (Portman).

05 Portman (Padmé) was pleased to work with Ewan McGregor (Obi-Wan Kenobi) in some emotional scenes.

STAR WARS: REVENGE OF THE SITH SPECIAL

BLUE SKY THINKING

BLUE SKY THINKING

Nothing would exist in the diverse and exotic *Star Wars* galaxy without the boundless imagination of the concept artists who worked together to develop new environments, costumes, and creatures for the saga. *Revenge of the Sith* was their most complex project to date.

tar Wars: Revenge of the Sith concept artist Iain McCaig was not sure that picking a film apart to tell who did what was a good thing. "It defeats the collaborative nature of the enterprise," he said. McCaig's words struck a theme heard repeatedly when *Star Wars Insider* talked with five concept artists about their work on the final movie in the prequel trilogy. While the artists interviewed—Ryan Church, Sang Jun Lee, Ian McCaig, Erik Tiemens, and Derek Thompson—were rightfully proud of their own creative contributions, they insisted that the real magic of the movie's concept art arose from their collective imagination.

It's revealing of the art department's team-oriented culture that McCaig, whose imaginative work led to some of the most memorable characters, creatures, and costumes of *The Phantom Menace* and *Attack of the Clones*, seemed reluctant to boast. "There were things that I designed which others inspired," he said. "And vice versa."

Indeed, inspiring others is what concept artists get paid to do, and chief among their job duties was to inspire *Star Wars*' head-of-everything, George Lucas.

The conceptual process began in pre-production in an atmosphere known at Skywalker Ranch as "Blue Sky." According to concept design supervisor Erik Tiemens, "Early on in pre-production, it was Ryan Church [the other concept design supervisor] and me coming up with ideas for different environments. That process served as a jumping off point for George."

Church, who designed many of the new alien cultures and technologies, said that those initial, script-less months were among his favorites because there were so few limitations. "Basically, the job was to try and wow George, and I was happy to oblige," he said.

At times, Lucas had a specific idea that he wanted rendered visually—a new Jedi starfighter or a new nemesis, for example—but he left other ideas wide open for the artists to flesh out. "He needed to have several planets for the Clone Wars to take place, along with the vehicles and droids on each world," recalled Church, who designed *Attack of the Clones*' main Geonosis ground battle vehicles: the AT-TE and the hailfire droid.

Church said he showed Lucas as much as he could during the early pre-production period. "I created illustrations that showed what I thought would be a cool shot in the movie scenarios, complete with settings, vehicles, characters—everything," he revealed. "It was so much fun that I'd constantly work late, making sure there was plenty to look at in our weekly meetings."

As ideas began to take shape, a crew of concept artists, model makers, and sculptors joined Church and Tiemens (this group included Robert Barnes, John Goodson, T.J. Frame, Warren Fu, Feng Zhu, Alex Jaeger, Michael Murnane, and Danny Wagner). Each week their task was to create a concept for a specific element or a design for the film.

"Most of the time we had four days to do concept work for a presentation to George on Friday morning," described concept artist Sang Jun Lee.

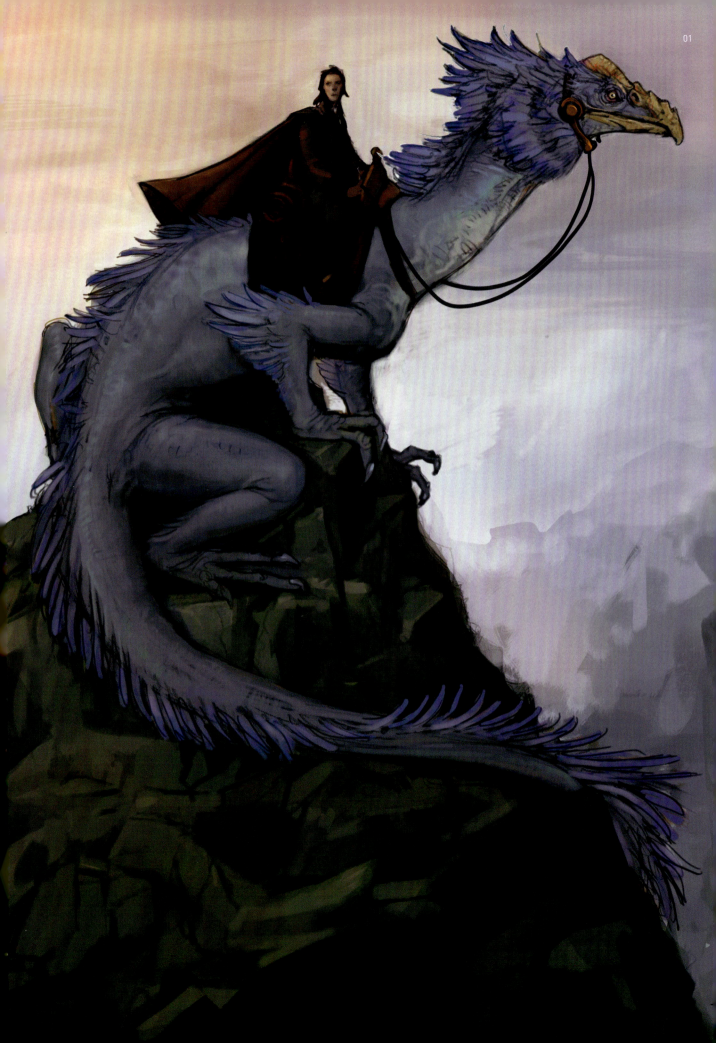

As before, sometimes Lucas didn't give the artists much to go on, while other times he was very specific. McCaig explained, "If it's one of the times you know that George is looking for input, you go as boldly as you dare, throwing out *your* worst nemesis, or *your* most bizarre universe."

Lee, who specialized in character and creature design, described his typical pre-production work week. "The first two days I spent on rough sketches and finding good references for new ideas," he said. "And then I started to draw detail sketching from the rough sketch or references to produce seven to fifteen drawings. On the last day I scanned the drawings and worked on painting them with Adobe Photoshop and Painter."

Lee's use of both traditional and digital tools was common in the art department. Many artists started with traditional materials to get their basic ideas down on paper, and then scanned their work into the computer for digital fine-tuning. Lee typically started with ink for his rough sketches and used a Prismacolor or graphite pencil for the detailed drawings. Once the drawings were in his computer, Photoshop let him block general shapes, or Painter allowed him to detail those shapes and add textures.

However, some artists developed a distinct preference for either traditional or electronic methods. "I'm pretty much a Luddite," admitted artist Derek Thompson, whose work was largely storyboards and keyframe art. Thompson, who came from a comic-book background, favored pencil, pen and marker. "I enjoy working electronically," he said. "But I found I can accomplish a lot with traditional means."

Others, like Church and Tiemens, worked electronically from the get-go. "Drawing and painting on the computer is so fast that there's really no barrier between me and the painting," said Church. "I use an electronic pen and tablet that lets me work exactly as I would with traditional media. It's completely intuitive and very fast, and I can try variations very easily. The program I use lets me paint quicker and more experimentally than I ever could with real paint."

As an artist, Tiemens found working electronically allowed for "more of a direct flow from what you're imagining. When you're painting traditionally, you have to be more careful and thoughtful. The materials can become a barrier to getting a concept done. In film, we've got a short deadline, and the artwork is really about conveying an idea, a concept, or the lighting and color, and that kind of thing. The actual process of crafting becomes less of an issue."

Whether they are created by electronic or traditional means, the designs and drawings at this stage are often very informal, barely more than sketches. "A great deal of my work is really gritty and foundational," said Thompson. "Intended to get the idea across and not so much about a pretty final image. And I'm talking rudimentary Post-It note sketches, large quantities of them."

Church said that he would approach new assignments intuitively: "I'll close my eyes and think about it for a minute or so and start drawing shapes, just making darks and lights on the page."

The work sometimes began with informal brainstorming sessions. As Tiemens recalled, "We'd get together around tables and brainstorm and joke, laugh, and bring books and point out movies. Things like that really got our sessions unlocked and flowing." But while all this freewheeling playtime was fun for the artists,

02

03

STAR WARS: REVENGE OF THE SITH SPECIAL

BLUE SKY THINKING

04

it was also important to the task at hand. Their freeform sessions were crucial for producing the highly imaginative and detailed worlds, creatures, vehicles, characters, and costumes that Star Wars fans love.

The art department's congenial environment did not occur accidentally—it was by design. As on all things Star Wars, the ultimate designer was George Lucas. The Revenge of the Sith artists were passionate in their praise of their boss, and seemed deeply grateful for the director's emphasis on collaboration and mutual inspiration.

"George Lucas is probably the most collaborative director I've ever known," confirmed McCaig, who treasured the concept artists' non-hierarchical camaraderie. "When the artists and designers came together, everyone's creative input was valued," he said.

"On Revenge of the Sith, I continued to work as I had since the first prequel movie: in close collaboration with my colleagues, but responsible only to George," McCaig added. "The fact that there were two officially titled concept design supervisors, a production designer, and a costume designer, creates the impression of a hierarchy that for me did not exist."

Although many ideas initially originated in Lucas' imagination, when it came to crystalizing them into usable concepts, he was a true collaborator with the artists. "It's really fun to interact with George and show him ideas and get his input," said Church. "There's always something refreshing—a different way of seeing, and the combination of things that he brings to the table that's illuminating."

Something else Church cherished was the creative freedom Lucas encouraged, and even demanded. "When an idea came from George, usually he'd tell me what he was thinking, like 'this character needs a speeder,' or 'that guy's base is on this type of planet.' But sometimes he would say 'design an interesting location for a battle,' or something else non-specific. That was great fun, and I was surprised by how hard he would push for something completely new. He'd be the first one to notice if I was being too conservative with my design. It's so fulfilling as a designer to be pushed that hard by your boss."

Such a high level of freedom was unusual in the entertainment-art world, according to Lee, who, like many of the concept team, had worked as an artist for several other films, including Men in Black II (2002), The Hulk (2003), and Peter Pan (2003). "I'm used to hearing from other directors exactly what they want, but George was more open to letting us present our own ideas before he started to specify what he wanted. It brought more responsibility and opportunity to the artist."

01 Previous page: Varactyl concept art by Sang Jun Lee.

02 Anakin Skywalker costume concept by Iain McCaig.

03 A study of Padmé Amidala by Iain McCaig.

04 Concept art for the opening space battle by Erik Tiemens.

STAR WARS: REVENGE OF THE SITH | 35

STAR WARS: REVENGE OF THE SITH SPECIAL

BLUE SKY THINKING

05

05 Clone troopers attack the Utapau sinkhole. Concept art by Erik Tiemens.

06 A mustafar creature concept by Derek Thompson.

Still, as Thompson pointed out, "It was a fun responsibility."

Perhaps Lucas worked so well with artists because he is, fundamentally, an artist himself. "It's great to work for someone who really values art and design and lets you know it," Church said. But like any artist, the director had some unusual methods, and inspiration could strike at any time.

Lee recalled a day when Lucas phoned the art department excitedly from his car. "He was driving down the street in San Francisco and came up with an idea for a creature. At that instant, he called us on his cell phone to give us direction for the type of character that he wanted to use."

At the Friday meetings, Lucas often singled out an element from an illustration for approval: a vehicle, a droid, or an architectural detail. But when the director approved an entire illustration, it could really thrill an artist. "When George got inspired by a piece of art that I created, it was a good day," Lee remembered.

Element by element, illustration by illustration, the look of each sequence in the film came into focus. The conceptual process was like putting together a jigsaw puzzle, and ultimately the art formed what Tiemens called a "visual script," which the film crew used as a guide when shooting. These paintings answered questions and resolved details about each sequence, some of which audiences might barely notice, such as what time of day it should be, the nature and direction of the lighting, and what kind of weather might be occurring.

One of the challenges of concept artwork is that it must often convey a huge amount of story, character development, and other information in what might ultimately amount to only a few seconds of screen time.

"For this film, the designs had to be extremely strong," said Church. "My approach to designing is based on the fact that you have to know a lot of information at just a glance. Does this object or location belong to the good guys or the bad guys? Which species does it belong to? How does this thing work? Is this a safe place or a dangerous place? Good, bold design can help answer these questions and therefore help tell the story. That's why most of my designs start as lit, colored paintings, so I can best see how the subject will look *in the movie* and not just on a white page."

Because the story was not finalized at this point, putting the big picture together became a delicious challenge for the art team, especially since the artists were typically assigned to work on one isolated piece of the puzzle at a time.

36 | STAR WARS: REVENGE OF THE SITH

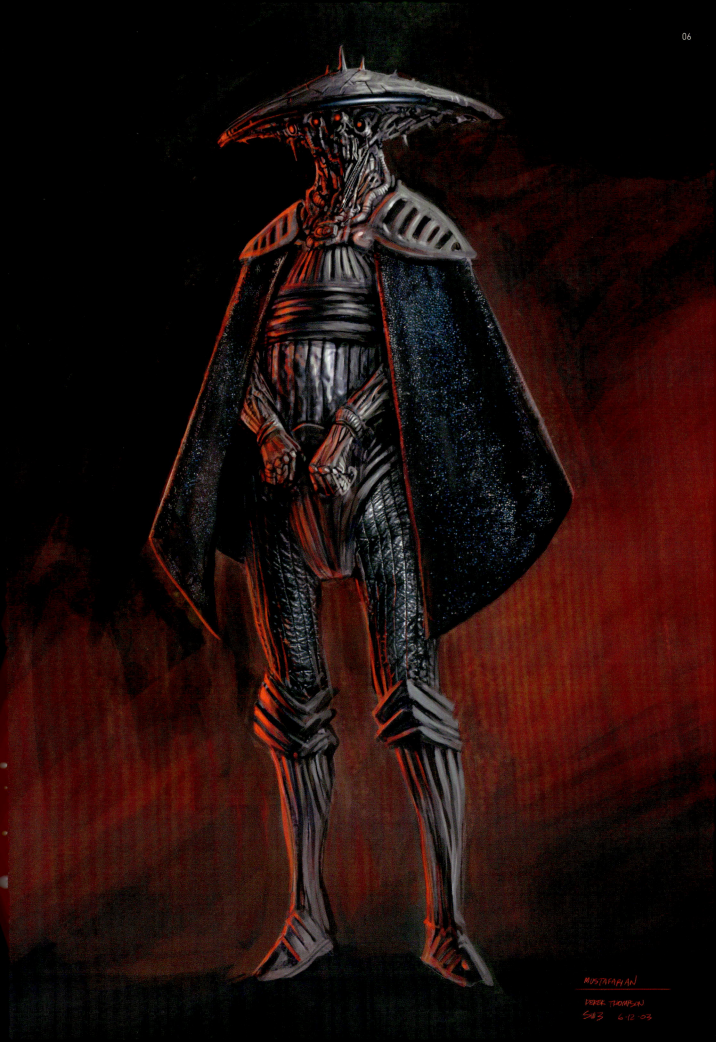

MUSTAFARIAN
DEREK THOMPSON
SW3 6-12-03

07

McCaig admitted that each artist couldn't help trying to get inside Lucas' head, to "see the movie through his eyes," but that wasn't easy. "It should have been a lot easier this time around," he reflected, "since we were finishing rather than starting the puzzle. However, looking for those last few pieces that actually fit was maddening *because* we were so close to seeing the big picture."

As Lucas approved elements and illustrations at the weekly meetings, the artists began to get a sense of what kinds of things appealed to him. From there, it was a process of designing scenes in detail and refining existing designs for the animatics department and Industrial Light & Magic to use in building models and creating fully rendered shots. However, the artists' work wasn't necessarily over when they'd worked out the concept bugs and ILM got in the game, partly because such bugs are never completely worked out. Tiemens suggested that the terms "pre-production" and "post-production" are misleading because making a film is seldom a linear process.

"It was weird, because we'd get into this middle zone of 'Wow, something needs to get reshot,' or George might have decided he had this whole other idea for a sequence and scrapped an earlier idea, and so we'd do a little pre-production, even in post-production. That happened a bit on *Attack of the Clones* with the droid factory and even the end battle. They weren't really locked down until much later."

"A film is really like a sketchbook that's filled with collages that you're looking at again to see how it all comes together and how each page contrasts with the other pages," Tiemens added.

"The biggest challenge was simply the huge amount of work required to design a movie of that scale," said Church. "My goal on *Revenge of the Sith* was to live up to the extremely high standards set by the other films. That was the biggest daily challenge about my job, but also the source of my greatest satisfaction. There was just so much to do and seemingly so little time to do it in!"

Lee agreed. "Every day you had to keep bringing new and unique ideas. In one year, we created more than 5,000 pieces of concept art for the movie. In all my years of working in this industry, I had never seen this amount of artwork for one feature film."

Another challenge for the art department was providing

07 "Crystal World" concept art by Sang Jun Lee.

08 Ship concept by Ryan Church.

38 | STAR WARS: REVENGE OF THE SITH

STAR WARS: REVENGE OF THE SITH SPECIAL

BLUE SKY THINKING

a visual bridge between the prequels and *A New Hope*. In McCaig's case, those bridges were major characters in the story. "Helping Anakin [Skywalker] and Obi-Wan [Kenobi] age and transform was a designer's delight," he said. "But Padmé [Amidala]'s final incarnation was one of the most emotional, creative challenges I've ever had to face."

Naturally, the artists were delighted when a concept they proposed made it into the final film with few changes, and several of the locations Church came up with during the "blue sky" phase of design "went through to final without modification," he said. "As have many of my vehicles, droids, and other designs. That was very gratifying."

Tiemens marveled at how fast the time flew from concept to final cut. "The most amazing thing is that you can be so intimate with a shot that you designed, and then when the movie comes out, and it really works with the music, the scoring, and the sound effects, on a large scale, it's very impressive," he says.

In the end, all five artists seemed most pleased with their collective work. "I am proud to have been a part of this saga," confirmed McCaig. "It meant a lot to me to see the story through to its end. It is always a pleasure and an honor to be invited into the creative process for *Star Wars*."

Tiemens, who remembered begging for a *Star Wars* sketch book when he was a boy, agreed. "All of us had those kinds of stories," he admitted, "and so we're seeing that inspiration come full circle." He mused, "I think the bottom line is that more of us should share in the act of being creative on team projects. It's just exhilarating. I think it uplifts everything."

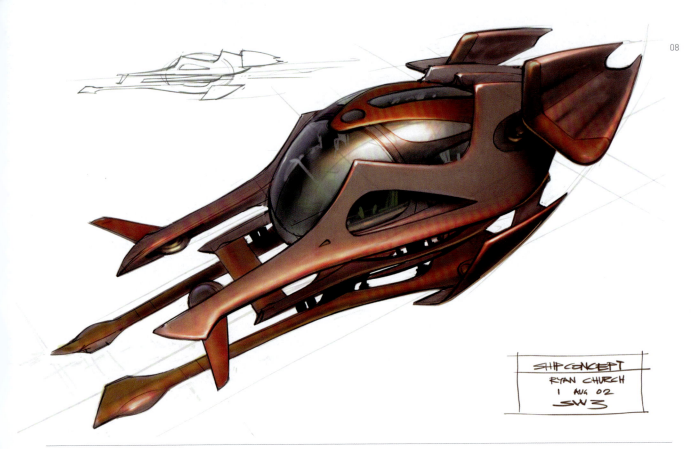

08

STAR WARS: REVENGE OF THE SITH | 39

THE HIGH GROUND
EWAN McGREGOR: OBI-WAN KENOBI

When they first met, Obi-Wan Kenobi had been wary of young Anakin Skywalker, the boy from Tatooine whom Qui-Gon Jinn insisted was the Chosen One. After taking Anakin on as his apprentice, training him to the best of his ability, the two formed a bond that was almost familial. The last thing that Kenobi imagined was that his brother would betray all for which they had fought together.

"If anything, *Revenge of the Sith* is more like the original trilogy than the other two films," Obi-Wan Kenobi actor Ewan McGregor said about the third prequel shortly before the picture's release. "In *The Phantom Menace*, for example, we had a lot of work to do to establish the plot and set up the saga as a whole, such as introducing the idea of the Senate and the Jedi. And even though we knew what the Jedi were, we saw them after their collapse, so we had to show what it was like when they were the Knights of the galaxy. *Attack of the Clones*, in turn, was very melodramatic. Now, in the latest film, there's nonstop action. Because it's the last film, we've really pulled out all the stops, no holds barred."

A third outing in the role originated by Sir Alec Guinness in the original trilogy afforded McGregor the opportunity to explore the character more deeply than his predecessor. "In the prequels, we've been able to learn more about Kenobi, whereas in the original films he was only really in the first half of the first movie, but it all goes back to Sir Alec," explained McGregor. "I feel my job was very easy—I just had to think about Alec Guinness and how he played his scenes in *A New Hope*. The choices he made for the character are still his today. I've been lucky to step into his shoes."

McGregor's resemblance to Guinness' Kenobi was pushed further for the film, much to the actor's delight. "It's been more important this time around than in the other films to get an Alec Guinness look and feel," McGregor confirmed. "Initially there was talk of wigs, but I thought my natural hair was quite like Alec's, so I got away with having his haircut. I've passed the mullet, which I sported beautifully in the last movie, to Hayden [Christensen], who carries the mullet flame through to the end."

The final chapter in the prequel trilogy saw the kinship between Kenobi and Anakin Skywalker (played by Christensen) collapse as the younger Jedi turned to the dark side of the Force. Conversely, the friendship that had grown between the two actors over the shooting of the two previous movies helped inform their characters' connection.

"Hayden and I are in the film a lot, and it was nice because we get along so well," remarked McGregor. "We actually created a relationship on screen that mimics our relationship off screen. What I enjoyed about this film specifically was that we had more to work out together. There are a lot of scenes with heavy dialogue where we really had to knuckle our heads together to make them work. We gave Obi-Wan and Anakin a bond that needed to be there in order to make the original trilogy work."

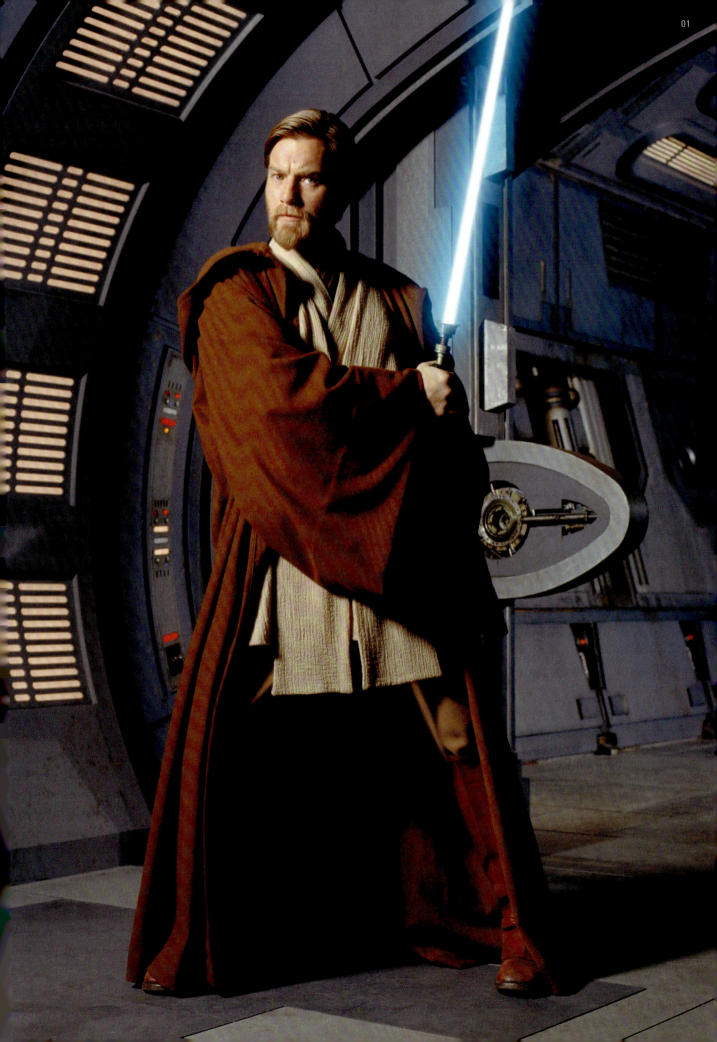

STAR WARS: REVENGE OF THE SITH SPECIAL
THE HIGH GROUND

Beyond the acting challenges of the script were the physical, as McGregor was once again called upon to wield a lightsaber, this time in a kinetic and extended duel with Christensen.

"I am very happy with all the fighting scenes, even though they were incredibly exhausting to do, and there were so many of them," McGregor confessed. "Hayden and I were constantly filming, one scene right after another, at such a fast pace. When I filmed *The Phantom Menace*, I'd fight all day long. I didn't care. It was like, 'Let's do more!' Now that I'm a bit older, it was more, 'OK guys, I think that's it. I've reached my limit.' I really noticed how much my stamina had decreased in that respect. It took about two weeks for my style to come back, because my body had to remember what it was like. Plus, there were an enormous amount of moves to learn, and none of the fighting was improvised. That would have been too dangerous. We had to perform each move to such a degree where we didn't have to think about them. Because we were moving so quickly, our bodies had to remember where the next cut was coming from. It all had to be fluid."

For McGregor, the circle was completed when filming scenes on the set of the *Tantive IV*, famous as Princess Leia's starship in the original *Star Wars* movie.

"That was a trip to film," McGregor recalled. "I had a few moments while shooting *Revenge of the Sith* that took me back to my childhood, and both were while filming with Anthony Daniels. Being on that set with C-3PO made me remember what it was like to be seven years old and watching the original films, and I felt the excitement of being in the prequels. I was also in a scene with R2-D2, and I found myself quite choked up about it, about this robot. It was quite a moment."

02

03

STAR WARS: REVENGE OF THE SITH SPECIAL

THE HIGH GROUND

01 Previous page: Ewan McGregor as Obi-Wan Kenobi.

02 Filming the Jedi Knight's rematch with Count Dooku.

03 Obi-Wan Kenobi (McGregor) prepares to take on General Grievous.

04 Obi-Wan Kenobi discovers the dreadful truth about Anakin.

05 McGregor (as Kenobi, right) and Christensen (as Skywalker, left) worked hard to give their characters a convincing bond.

06 Filming on a set he remembered from *A New Hope* was a "trip" for McGregor.

STAR WARS: REVENGE OF THE SITH | 43

STAR WARS: REVENGE OF THE SITH SPECIAL

KEEPING THE PEACE

KEEPING THE PEACE
SAMUEL L. JACKSON: MACE WINDU

A leading member of the Jedi Council, Mace Windu had reservations about Anakin Skywalker's suitability for training in the Jedi arts from their very first meeting. Those feelings, combined with his unease over the prophecy of the Chosen One, persisted until the fateful day that Anakin learned the identity of the secret Sith Lord behind the Clone Wars, and turned on Windu and the entire Jedi Order.

The prospect of playing out Mace Windu's final moments in *Revenge of the Sith* was not a problem for renowned screen actor Samuel L. Jackson. "I'm feeling pretty great about it," he revealed to *Star Wars Insider* prior to the movie's 2005 release. "I have a good sense of satisfaction. It's a satisfying death!"

Windu plunged to his demise, pushed through a window by Anakin Skywalker, following a lightsaber duel with Supreme Chancellor Palpatine. "I've always wanted to be this kind of Errol Flynn-like swashbuckler, from the time I was, like, two or three years old," Jackson revealed. "My friends and I would take sticks and sword fight through trees, off our porches, down hills, and everywhere else—it's almost like I've practiced for this death scene all my life!"

The fight with Palpatine, choreographed by stunt coordinator Nick Gillard, was therefore a dream come true for the actor. "Nick and I had been talking about it for a few years," said Jackson. "He's combined a lot of different fighting styles, so it looks very good. It's spectacular. It shows off my skills, and many sides of Mace Windu during the fight: it makes him look dominant, it makes him vulnerable, it makes him sneaky in many ways, and it makes him strong. Nick is a kind, gentle taskmaster, and he's tried to find things that are unique to me [and] make Mace this interesting sort of fighter who is very at ease yet very lethal."

Famously, Windu used a lightsaber with a very individual purple blade, first wielded in *Attack of the Clones*. "One day, I just asked George Lucas if I could have a different colored lightsaber. He asked me what color I wanted, so I said 'Purple,'" Jackson recalled. "He asked me why, and I said, 'Well, I just want a different color because [Mace] is high up on the Jedi Council and has a bit more power, second to Yoda, and I think I should have a different color.' George said there were only two colors, but that he would think about it. When I came back later, he said he had something to show me and there it was. George said it was just an experiment for the moment, but somehow or other, even though he had done it as an experiment, it was already on the Internet. People began wondering what it all meant. 'Mace has a purple lightsaber?!' It was nothing. I asked and he said 'Okay.'"

Would it be fair to suggest that Mace Windu and Samuel L. Jackson aren't such dissimilar characters? "I'm bold, I'm black. He's bold, he's black. I know everything, he knows everything. Let me think…" the actor paused, feigning deep thought. "Not much. Not very much! (*laughs*) I'm pretty even-tempered, he's pretty much even-tempered. I guess we are a lot alike in certain ways. I mean, I actually try to make decisions rationally and not jump to conclusions!"

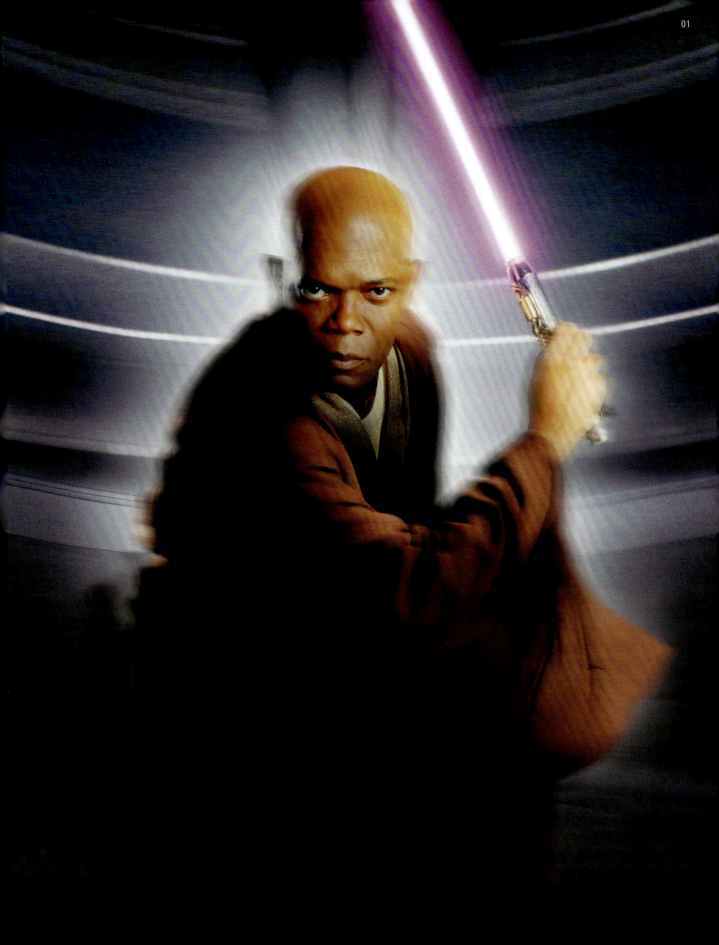

STAR WARS: REVENGE OF THE SITH SPECIAL
KEEPING THE PEACE

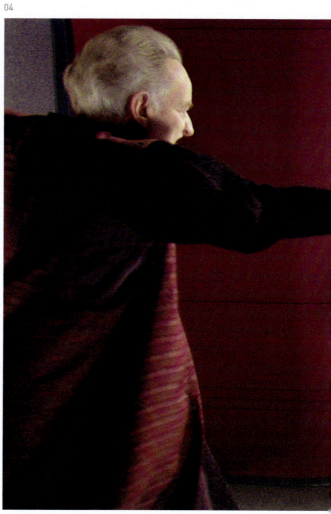

01 Previous page: Samuel L. Jackson as Mace Windu.

02 Mace Windu (Jackson) in the Jedi Council chamber.

03 Jackson felt Mace Windu should have a purple lightsaber to reflect his high rank on the Jedi Council.

04 Palpatine (Ian McDiarmid) duels with Windu (Jackson).

05 Director George Lucas (center) shows Jackson (right) a foamcore model of the Palpatine office set.

With extensive use of green and blue screens on set all the way through production of the prequel trilogy, actors were often required to use their imagination to visualize the scenes they were performing. From Jackson's perspective, that's what acting is all about.

"Definitely, as an actor, your imagination is key, especially in terms of characterization and what you're going to do, what you need to do, and what you want to become," he agreed. "If there's not a lot of information on the page about who you are, or if it's not written from some book, then you as an actor have free reign to create all kinds of things about who you are, what you want to look like, where you come from—all those things. You have a 'blue screen' of character development all around you, of things you want to say about yourself and who you want yourself to be. So, when you show up to start filming, you can ask a director if it's okay to be this, that, or the other."

Asked what it was that gave Star Wars its broad appeal, Jackson gave the idea some thought. "Everybody sees something different inside these films, such as the heroic, societal, and political aspects," he said. "The story itself is one we all know. It's like all morality tales, the good-versus-evil kind of thing. But it's still kind of tongue in cheek, because it's hard to tell what is good and what is bad. You get to make your own choices about that. As I read the story for Revenge of the Sith, I felt the Shakespearean aspects would cause a lot of debate among people. In the end, I love the way it all plays out.

"This story is a bit darker, and I'd say it's for the tweeners, it's for the adults who always wanted to know what happened, but really it's for kids. It's kind of like the Sleeping Beauty of the Star Wars set, because Sleeping Beauty is a very scary story for kids. This is also the film that explains a lot; it's going to be the one that balances the rest out. George has done an amazing job of putting it all together for the kids, teenagers, and adults. Everything is right there. George knows his audience, who they are, and he cares about them. He cares about the kids, and kids need stories that are for and about them."

STAR WARS: REVENGE OF THE SITH SPECIAL
KEEPING THE PEACE

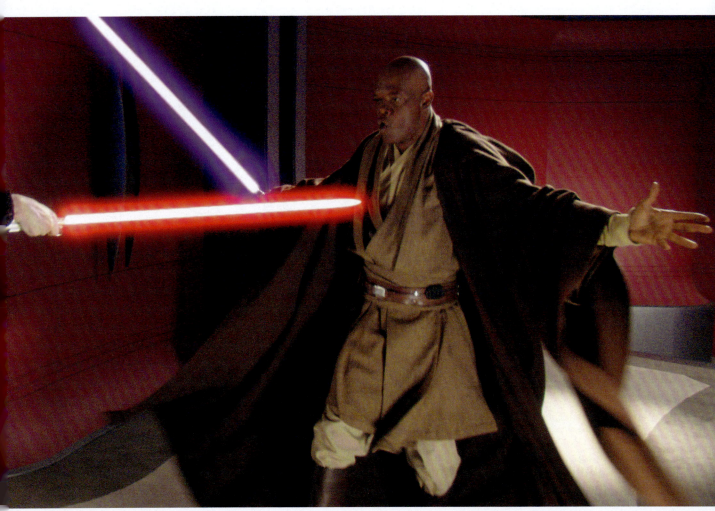

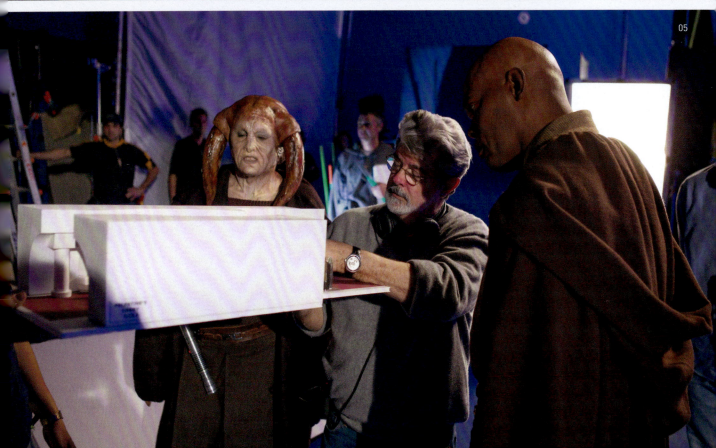

MATERIAL WORLDS

Just as important as the myriad of characters and creatures of *Star Wars: Revenge of the Sith*, the costumes that draped its mythic heroes and villains helped define who they were. Costume designer Tricia Biggar and her team faced the challenging task of weaving together an alluring and believable cinematic experience through the subtleties of fabric, color, and texture.

Having won several prestigious awards for her work on *Star Wars: The Phantom Menace* and *Attack of the Clones*, Tricia Biggar already had an eye for the look of the galaxy far, far away when she began developing ideas for *Revenge of the Sith* shortly after the theatrical release of Episode II.

"I began working on the project in August of 2002," Biggar explained. "I went up to Skywalker Ranch to have an initial meeting with George [Lucas] to talk about what he was envisioning for the various environments, and to see what the concept artists had started developing for those environments."

Biggar was impressed by the rich ideas the art department had come up with. "On something like *Star Wars*, you can find inspiration from any culture, any time. There are absolutely no limitations," she said, enthusiastically. "You can use anything from anywhere, and that's fantastic."

Despite running a smaller costume department than on the previous movies, the process of getting things up and running was easier the third time around. "It felt much less rushed, and it was much nicer to have the workshop in Sydney going for a longer period of time," Biggar confirmed. "I think between the costume department and costume props, we had about eighty people. We were able to set up, get organized, and be ready to go by January of 2003."

The process of breaking down how many costumes would be needed for each of the main and supporting characters began before the shooting script was even finalized. "With a normal script, you work from a day-by-day breakdown, and in a way, we did the same thing with *Revenge of the Sith*," the costume designer elaborated. "Basically, for each planet that was seen, we broke down each into story days. For instance, on Coruscant, we would work out when it was morning, afternoon, evening, or even the next day, and then decide when to make a costume change. Usually, if it was the next day, the actor would get a change of clothes, unless there was a reason why they would be wearing the same costume. George had a very clear idea of what he wanted. Even if the script wasn't on paper, the storyline was in his head. Often, we would keep minor characters wearing the same costume. For the major characters, we could afford to change their clothes as often as necessary."

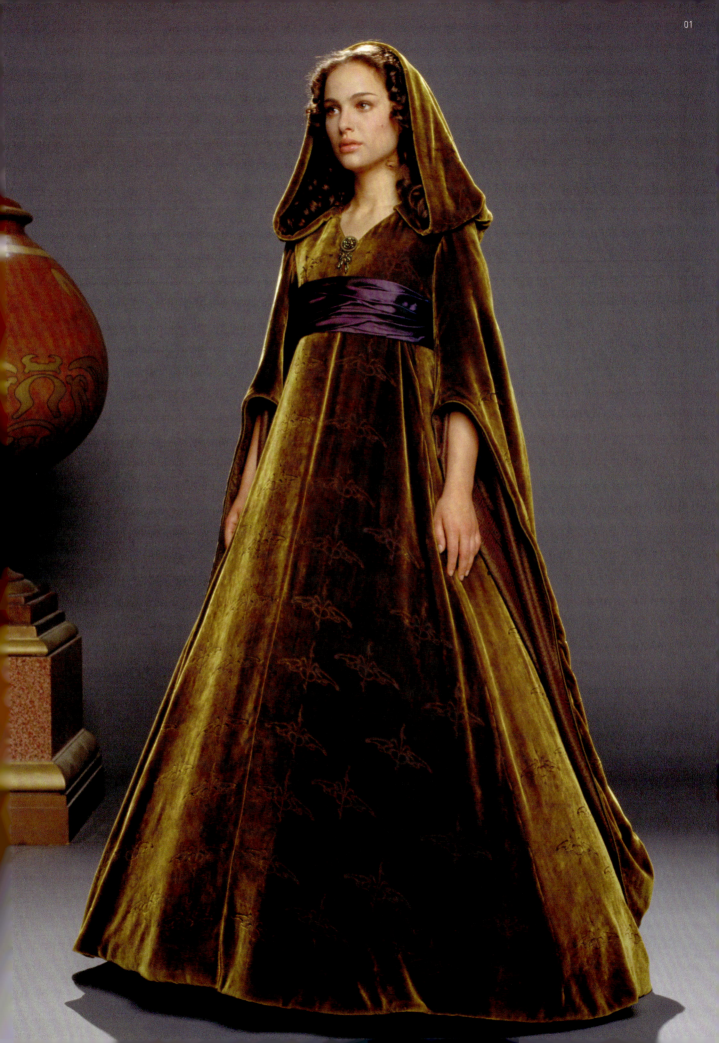

STAR WARS: REVENGE OF THE SITH SPECIAL
MATERIAL WORLDS

A fundamental component of each costume was the fabric used to make it. In a film set in a far distant galaxy, that could mean anything from simple canvas to intricate weaves or even bespoke cloths. Biggar's search for suitable materials went world-wide.

"We ended up using fabrics from everywhere," said Biggar. "In the U.S., we bought fabrics in Los Angeles, San Francisco, and New York. We also sourced a lot of fabrics from a big trade show in Paris that manufacturers from all over the world went to. From there, we ended up contacting agents in London from various manufacturers. We bought fabrics in Japan, China, and India. Again, all over the world. I also used a lot of vintage fabrics, which I sourced from many places, including Scotland, America, and France."

Not only did the resultant costumes need to look the part, they had to be suitable for the kind of action and stunts synonymous with the *Star Wars* movies. This often meant alternate but visually identical versions of the same costume had to be made for different shots.

"They had to be detailed very closely to the original costumes," confirmed Biggar. "For example, when creating the [regular] costumes for the Neimoidian gunners, we made them out of all sorts of fiberglass; the stunt versions were made out of a flexible material. Whereas for Palpatine's stunt attire, we used exactly the same fabric as we did for Ian McDiarmid's costumes. They were complete copies, but we allowed for extra padding to be worn underneath by the stunt man. We also made some lightweight cloaks for Obi-Wan Kenobi's water scenes (later cut from the movie), which involved using metal weights to fit into different parts of the garment to keep them from becoming like a parachute and floating up."

02

01 Previous page: Every outfit in Padmé Amidala's wardrobe was designed to disguise the character's pregnancy.

02 Hundreds of costumes were required for all the background actors in the movie.

03-04 Padmé Concept art by IainMcCaig.

With numerous shots involving pyrotechnics, there were also safety considerations, including fireproofing. "We would give samples of the fabrics to the special effects team to be burn-tested," Biggar revealed. "They would separate the costumes into sections and give them back to us to be fireproofed. We would then turn them around for a second test. In some cases, we would have to use a second coat of fireproofing. If you have pyrotechnics, obviously you have to make sure. We accomplished this by using a special spray solution that was safe for skin, because the entire costume had to be saturated."

A very specific requirement of the plot was that Padmé Amidala's pregnancy should remain a secret throughout the film, including in scenes where the character spent time undertaking her senatorial duties. "First off, George didn't want her to appear pregnant in any sort of public situation," said Biggar. "Only her handmaidens and Anakin would be aware. The difficulty was to create a shape for Padmé's costumes that looked natural and allowed for movement, like sitting and standing, so the people she was interacting with wouldn't know she was pregnant. We settled on a basic shape that worked quite well.

STAR WARS: REVENGE OF THE SITH SPECIAL

MATERIAL WORLDS

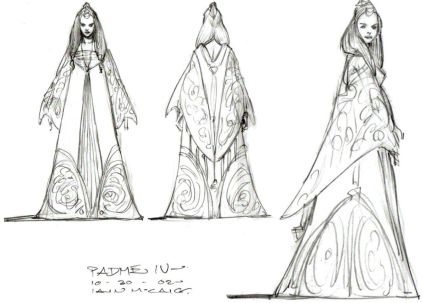

03 04

STAR WARS: REVENGE OF THE SITH | 51

STAR WARS: REVENGE OF THE SITH SPECIAL

MATERIAL WORLDS

05

06

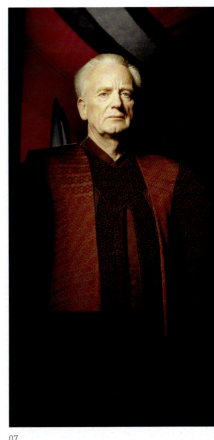

07

05 Palpatine had multiple wardrobe changes in Episode III.

06 Costume concept art by Sang Jun Lee.

07 The use of darker colors and more textures in Palpatine's costumes were intended to show the deterioration of his character as his evil persona began to reveal itself.

08 The iconic looks of the Emperor and Darth Vader were recreated for *Revenge of the Sith*.

"All of the costumes in which she is seen in public hung from the shoulder and were supported on what was, essentially, a simplified crinoline shape underneath," she continued. "Using steel rings in the petticoats, and quilted petticoats to keep stiffness underneath, let me use soft fabrics on the top, so there was still a very soft feminine feel to her costumes. For the bump, we ended up making a variety of different shapes to work under different outfits, for times when Padmé would be sitting rather than standing or walking, for example. We also made a modified bump when we wanted to see more of it, [to make the audience] more aware of it. All told, Padmé ended up with twelve costumes in this film."

Another character with multiple wardrobe changes in Episode III was Supreme Chancellor Palpatine, played by Ian McDiarmid. "It was quite interesting this time, because in Episode II Ian only had one or two costumes," said Biggar. "In Episode III, because of all the different situations we see him in—like fighting, escaping from a crashing spaceship, and so forth— Palpatine needed more outfits to show that his powers had increased. It was nice because we could use textures and lots of dark colors to show the audience the deterioration of his character. The first costume you saw him in, on the Trade Federation starship, was made of a kind of wool with a latex-type material over the top, which gave an almost crumbling, animal sort of feel to the fabric, and helped show his inner decay. Some of his costumes were quite elaborate. We used lots of velvets, embroidery, and printing to give his costume some extra depth. The last one, before he became the Emperor, was a sort of dark elephant gray, which in some lights looked black."

The icing on the cake was the opportunity to recreate the iconic Darth Vader costume for actor Hayden Christensen. "That costume was completely new," revealed Biggar. "We did very little to change the design from what was seen in the original trilogy, except we made the costume to fit Hayden. There were some things that we corrected, however, like the helmet. When the original was first sculpted, it was obviously done by hand, and one side of the face was slightly at an angle. We made it so it was symmetrical. It allowed Hayden a lot of extra head movement that wasn't possible before."

Biggar recalled when Christensen's Vader first walked onto the set. "That was a fantastic moment," she said. "For Hayden, it was huge because of the history of Darth Vader, but when he appeared it was just spine tingling."

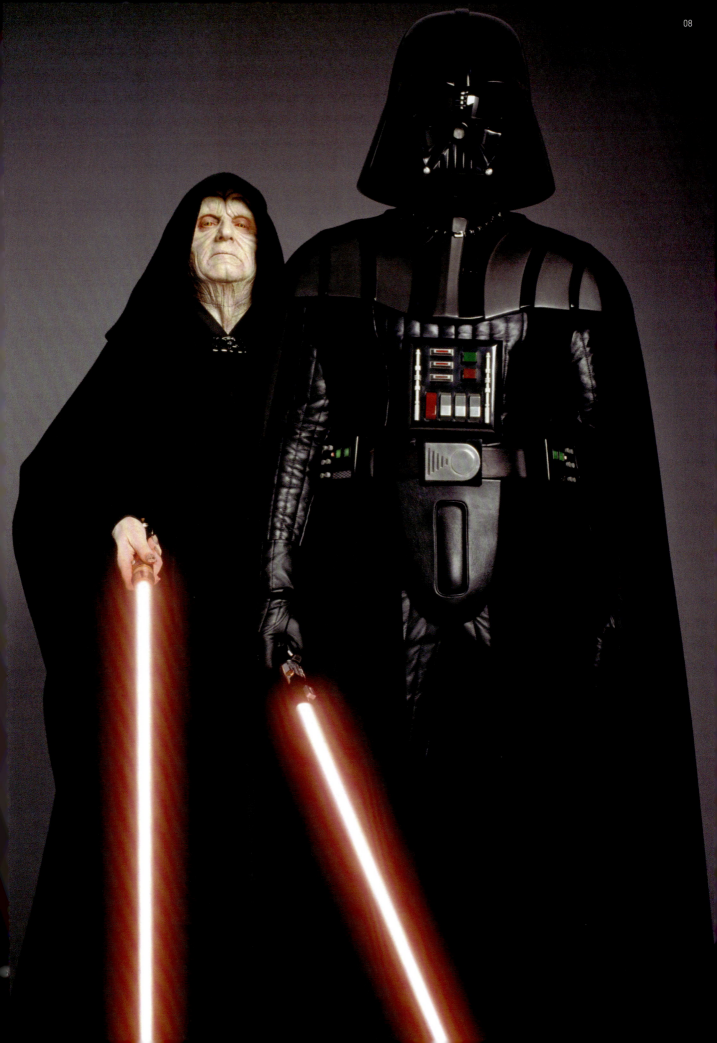

CREATING KASHYYYK

One of the earliest locales imagined for the galaxy far, far away was Kashyyyk, the home of the Wookiees, which was first mentioned in early story drafts for George Lucas' original movie. Planned to be the site of an immense ground battle, the concept was eventually dropped as the plot moved along a different path—*Revenge of the Sith* finally gave Lucas an opportunity to realize those plans.

01

Senior concept designers Ryan Church and Erik Tiemens were tasked with bringing the never-before-seen world of the Wookiees to life, and they began honing the look of Kashyyyk after concluding work on *Attack of the Clone*s. "As Clones was wrapping up, George [Lucas] said he needed a bunch of planets for the Clone Wars to be happening on and wanted to see what we could come up with," Church recalled. "We immediately asked if Kashyyyk could be one of them, and he said, 'Sure, show me something.' So, that first week I did a painting that showed a big leaning tree adorned with wooden architecture, hanging over a river with little waterfalls."

It was this early production phase that Church said was the most fun. "It's great when the director comes to you and asks you to just draw. At first, George didn't give us too many specifics. They came later. He just wanted to be wowed. As the process went on, he wanted to see something that was bigger and bigger and bigger. Over time, the first little piece I did evolved into something larger, but the core idea was the same," Church explained.

Being one of the senior concept designers, Church had an overall look in mind for Kashyyyk, and that vision extended beyond just an elaborate dwelling positioned over a body of water. "I knew I wanted to see something like Tahiti or Hawaii in Episode III, just because it was different than what we'd seen in any previous *Star Wars* films. I had envisaged a more tropical, sunlit

01 Wookiee tree interior concept art by Ryan Church.

STAR WARS: REVENGE OF THE SITH | 55

STAR WARS: REVENGE OF THE SITH SPECIAL

CREATING KASHYYYK

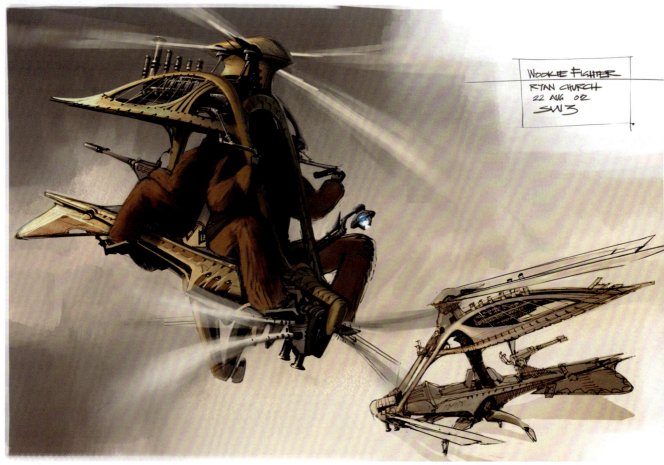

02

02 Ryan Church's concept for the Wookiee "dragonfly" aerial vehicle.

03 Modelmaker John Duncan working on the Kashyyyk tree set.

04 Wookiee tree concept art by Ryan Church.

05 Construction of the tree miniature in progress.

06 Modelmaker Danny Wagner sculpting the tree maquette.

planet," he said. Ultimately, this brighter concept for the planet's landscape would be toned down, still tropical but with a colder, more monochromatic feel in keeping with the look Lucas was going for with the entire movie.

The one thing that would distinguish Kashyyyk and the Wookiee culture from the rest of the planets and species in *Revenge of the Sith* was the cohesiveness of their society, which included their architecture and their technology. First and foremost, the Wookiees were technologically advanced and high tech in every way. They were not supposed to be primitive, which meant no torches or huts.

"I imagined that they would be like Frank Lloyd Wright—master craftsmen—and that their architecture would be brushed aluminum integrated into wood, similar to what you'd find in the interior of a nice luxury car," explained Church. "For some of the other planets in the film, George specifically wanted them to look like they were made by a bunch of different architects, whereas the Wookiee designs were very focused and didn't reflect a lot of history. Their style of architecture wasn't old or new, it was all its own thing. Very pure."

An area of the project Church particularly enjoyed was developing Wookiee vehicles, such as the airborne "dragonfly." Church revealed that he'd gained inspiration from the chrome and brushed-aluminum styling and all-wooden frames of speed boats from the 1930s. "The dragonfly was basically a flying motorcycle, but it had its own aesthetic. I wanted to make it so that the vehicle had all these weird control linkages, which very much resembled handlebars on a chopper, going from the front seat to the back," he said. "I thought it would be cool to see something in a *Star Wars* film that actually flapped." As for its crew, the dragonfly had enough space for two, which was a conscious decision by Church. "I imagined the pilots working as a team to actually keep the thing in the air," he recalled.

"George likes to show things very matter-of-factly, and it was my goal to make Kashyyyk a huge, grand place and make a statement the moment he saw it," said Church. "I wanted to create something I would have thought was cool when I was a kid, and I can't think of anything cooler than a city built around a thousand-foot-tall tree. It's like the ultimate treehouse."

STAR WARS: REVENGE OF THE SITH SPECIAL

CREATING KASHYYYK

Miniature World

Brian Gernand was the practical model supervisor for Industrial Light & Magic's Model Shop for *Revenge of the Sith* and oversaw turning the wealth of Kashyyyk concept art into the physical environs of the planet. Once the final designs had been approved, sculptor Danny Wagner made the first three-dimensional tree maquettes. Using these as reference, Gernand's twenty-strong team embarked upon the thirteen-week task of crafting a 1:72-scale miniature tree that stood more than 12-feet tall. The massive and intricately detailed miniature would be shot from a multitude of angles and digitally inserted in different parts of the landscape, providing the illusion of a beach-fringing jungle forest.

"The tree was great. It was just a really fun thing to do," said Gernand. "It was clearly styled and conceptually very specific, and we worked closely with Erik Tiemens and Ryan Church to determine how we were going to build it.

"The basic tree started out as a giant foam sculpture," he continued, explaining how Wagner's prototype maquette was scaled up. "To replicate the exact shape, we cut it up into sections and blew those profiles up on a printer to the diameter that we needed for our scale." The final miniature was based around a supporting steel armature, over which foam rings, cut to scale from the enlarged profile prints, gave the modelmakers the tree's basic shape. "That was then detail-sculpted by our lead sculptor, Satjawatcharaphong Gritsada, and we transitioned it into this nice little section of ground and a beachfront."

The next step was to give the gargantuan tree its bark, which was achieved by applying clay to the model and carving in tree-like detail. "There were areas as if the bark had come off, and what you were looking at was the really smooth hardwood that would be underneath," added Gernand. "Once sculpted, it was painted with a finish that made it look more like bark. All the structures that went onto the tree were [made from] laser-cut, handlaid teak strips and metal banding, so all those platforms were actually metal and wood. Utterly gorgeous."

STAR WARS: REVENGE OF THE SITH SPECIAL

CREATING KASHYYYK

The Return of Chewbacca

While Kashyyyk was realized on screen through a mix of physical miniatures and digital environments, the planet needed one final, crucial element to bring it to life: Wookiees, and lots of them. Amidst the very tall Australian performers hired to fill the furry costumes on the Sydney set, a returning actor traveled halfway around the globe to reprise the role that had made Wookiees world famous in the first place.

"I got a phone call from Rick McCallum last year," recalled Peter Mayhew, who played Chewbacca in the original *Star Wars* trilogy, at the time. "He wanted to check on my availability. Of course, I said I wasn't available!" he laughed.

Joking aside, Mayhew confirmed that he had been more than happy to slip back inside a Wookiee costume. "Not only was it great personally to be able to become that character again, to bring him back after all this time, but it generally seemed to make people happy," he said. "Chewie is a very comforting character."

However, Mayhew would have to wait a while longer before filming his scenes as the famous "walking carpet" for *Revenge of the Sith*. The 57-day shoot that had taken place in 2003 had covered most of the movie's live-action scenes, but there were notable omissions.

Several major sequences that had been in the script since day one had been left off the principal photography schedule to be shot at a later date. Mayhew and seven new Wookiee performers were therefore recalled to Sydney in the Spring of 2004 to film the Battle of Kashyyyk, having already had their costume fittings the previous summer.

"As soon as I put the Chewie costume on, the character came out," remembered Mayhew. "It was like riding a bike. One minute I could be standing there talking to someone and having a normal conversation, but the moment I put on the mask, I became the character. Chewbacca literally came alive. It was quite amazing."

07 Peter Mayhew returned to play Chewbacca in *Revenge of the Sith*.

08 Chewbacca, Yoda, and General Tarfful in contact with the Jedi Council.

09 Mayhew as Chewbacca enjoying a blast of cool air on set.

10 Tarfful (Michael Kingma) and Chewbacca (Peter Mayhew).

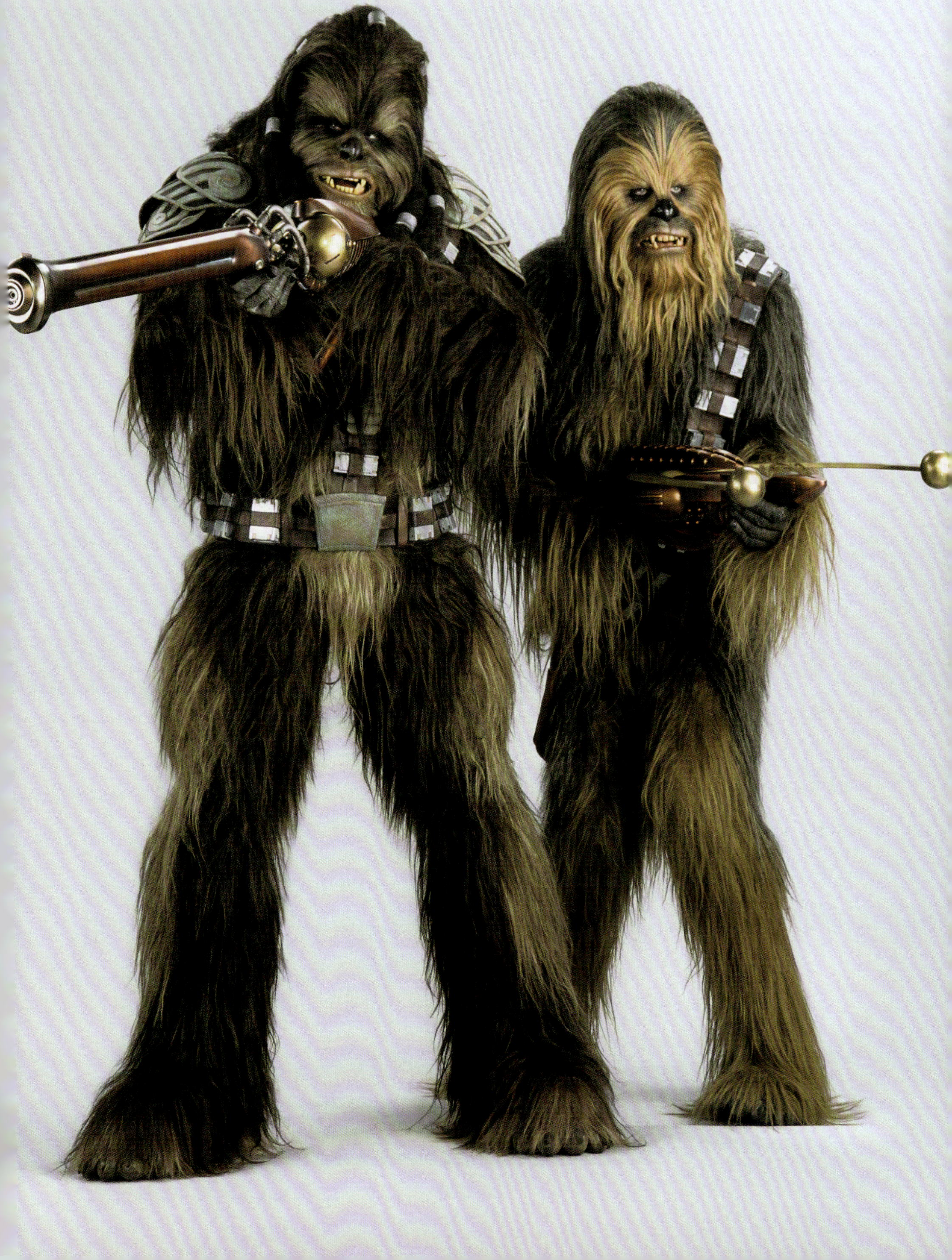

STAR WARS: REVENGE OF THE SITH SPECIAL
CREATING KASHYYYK

Mayhew also benefited from a new Chewie costume that made allowances for the heat of the Australian climate. While faithful in design to the original, albeit with muscle padding to indicate this was a younger Wookiee, the new costume featured an arterial cooling system underneath the fur. "On the original costume, there was no ventilation system at all," confirmed Mayhew. "I would be fortunate if there was a big fan on set. For the new suit, there were two tubes wrapped around my body that could be plunged into an ice pack with cold water in it. The pack itself was detachable, so it could be hooked up to have cool water pumped through the tubes whenever there was a break, which kept me relatively cool."

With Chewbacca's scenes being quieter, character moments alongside Yoda (digitally added later), the other Wookiee performers had a more physical time as they shot live-action footage for the main battle.

"Axel Dench was their leader of sorts," remarked Creature Shop Supervisor Rebecca Hunt. Axel, a basketball player, portrayed an imposing Wookiee bedecked in armor and braids. "In one of his takes, he got so into it he received a round of applause from the crew," Hunter recalled. "I think, after that, some of the other Wookiees started looking to get that kind of recognition."

11 The new Wookiee costumes for *Revenge of the Sith* included a foam musculature.

12 Strands of yak hair were painstakingly applied to each Wookiee mask.

STAR WARS: REVENGE OF THE SITH SPECIAL

CREATING KASHYYYK

Digital Wookiees

Despite putting everything into their performances, it would take more than this handful of human players to populate Kashyyyk, with its lagoon-side tree cities, both teeming with warriors and civilians. For some of the most crowded battle scenes, animation was used to fill the frame with digital Wookiee extras.

The motion-capture stage became a workout room for Michael Kingma, the six-foot-eleven Australian basketball player recruited for the live-action role of Tarfful. For this part of the shoot, Kingma wore quite a different outfit—a tight spandex suit covered with little reflective balls. "He's playing every digital Wookiee," said Doug Griffin of ILM's motion-capture department.

On a small stage surrounded by a complex array of sixteen perfectly calibrated cameras, Griffin often performed the moves himself before directing Kingma. Reference material was on hand to help the actor further visualize what was required of him, including a laptop playing footage from *A New Hope*. Scenes of Chewbacca loping through the Death Star revealed a pretty relaxed Wookiee trot, for example. Data captured by the cameras turned the reflective balls on Kingma's bodysuit into a digital wireframe humanoid that could be viewed from any angle, replaying his every move. These would eventually be adapted and applied to multiple computer-generated Wookiees.

Kingma worked hard as nameless Wookiee extras leading troops into the fray, jumping out from behind cover and charging forward, or recoiling from heavy ordnance. Doing motion capture may have been easier than running around in a full Wookiee outfit, but it was still a tough job.

13 Concept art of the Wookiee counter attack by Aaron McBride.

14-15 Multiple live-action plates were shot against a blue screen and combined with digitial Wookiees for the final shot.

13

14

15

STAR WARS: REVENGE OF THE SITH | 61

UNLIMITED POWER

IAN McDIARMID: SUPREME CHANCELLOR PALPATINE

Declaring himself Galactic Emperor during the final moments of *Revenge of the Sith* was the culmination of a plan Sheev Palpatine had been nurturing for decades. The secret Sith Lord had manipulated entire star systems into a devastating war, corrupted the Senate, and discredited the Jedi Order. Ultimate power was finally in his grasp.

"I think you'd probably be a very strange person indeed if you didn't know that I played Darth Sidious and Palpatine, although of course I never admitted it in public," Ian McDiarmid intimated to *Insider*. "There are no credits for Darth Sidious, but anyone who's seen *Return of the Jedi* and heard that voice, seen this 'nose' (*laughs*), all those things. They knew it was me. All sorts of complicated reasons could be evinced for suggesting I was playing two characters, but of course he was always the one person."

The actor, who played the Emperor in the original *Star Wars* trilogy, received some useful advice on the duality of the Palpatine role from director George Lucas while shooting *The Phantom Menace*. "He said, 'In a sense, your eyes are contact lenses.' In other words, the Palpatine character was artificial, because the real Palpatine was the one who burst forth at a calculated moment in *Revenge of the Sith*, just after persuading Anakin to kill Mace Windu," McDiarmid explained. "That was when the true person came out, letting the evil fully manifest itself. The Emperor looked like he did because he was very old and very evil, but that was what he had always looked like. He'd just had this carapace of looking like a fairly ordinary guy; a politician that smiled a bit, and so on."

Conversely, McDiarmid's affable face was covered with prosthetics and makeup to bring forth Palpatine's evil visage. "Creature shop designer Dave Elsey, who designed the prosthetic and applied it, created something that was relatively easy to wear," the actor recalled. "It was a two-hour makeup call every day, but by the end Dave and Colin Ware got it down to about an hour and a half. It took about the same length of time to take it off. When it was first applied, several people had a sort of metaphorical heart attack, so I thought, 'Oh good, it's working!'"

A major throughline of the prequel trilogy was Palpatine's interest in Anakin Skywalker, and McDiarmid was pleasantly surprised to see that theme feature prominently in the *Revenge of the Sith* script. "I was knocked out by the fact that George [Lucas] focused so much on the relationship between Anakin and Palpatine," he revealed. "Certainly in action film terms, they really were enormous dialogue scenes. It was daunting.

"The scene at the opera is probably one of the longest dialogue scenes that I've ever done, and it's just two people talking to each other, listening and reacting, during which Palpatine offers all sorts of tidbits, hints, and possibilities to Anakin, waiting to see which one he'll pick up. It was great and courageous of George to take that risk in a film where everybody was waiting to see the next action sequence."

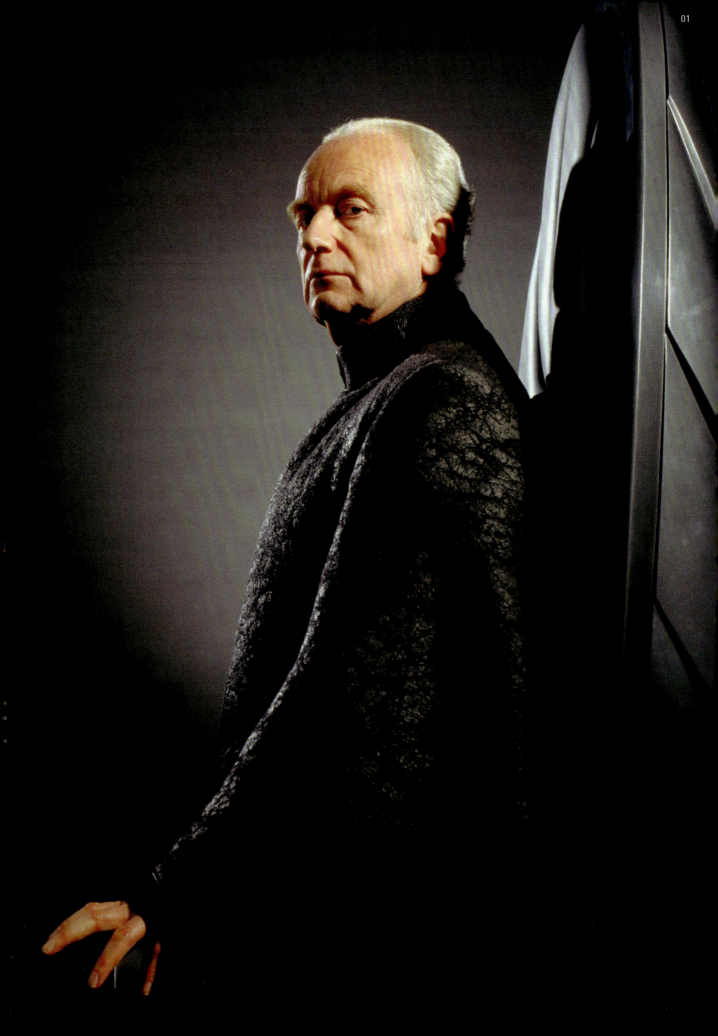

STAR WARS: REVENGE OF THE SITH SPECIAL
UNLIMITED POWER

01 Previous page: Ian McDiarmid as Supreme Chancellor Palpatine.

02 Palpatine (McDiarmid) showed his true colors when confronted by Mace Windu.

03 Darth Sidious (McDiarmid) enacting Order 66.

04 McDiarmid spent two hours in makeup to be transformed into Darth Sidious.

05 Ian McDiarmid as Darth Sidious.

The actor also shared his thoughts on the subtlety of Palpatine's long-term plan to seduce Anakin to the dark side of the Force. "Palpatine cultivated this friendship over the years since he first gave Anakin a friendly tap on the shoulder in *The Phantom Menace*," he said. "The interesting thing is that the temptation had to be—from Anakin's point of view, and therefore the audiences— convincing. I had to find a way of working with Hayden Christensen to make this whole political seduction believable, which wasn't difficult because he was great. The temptation had to be convincing, real, and desirable, even though at the end of the day one would hope that you wouldn't succumb, because the ends are obvious.

"With Anakin, although he wouldn't admit it early on or even realized it, he wanted the power," the actor added. "It wasn't like an evil genius was needed to plant an evil seed or an evil gene. The seed was already there, and the evil genius just helped it to grow. I'm confident that, mainly because of Hayden's wonderful performance, the audience will think, 'Yes, I suppose that could happen to me.'"

McDiarmid believed that, despite Palpatine being the most manipulative, vile being in the galaxy, he did care for Anakin—in his own way. "There is one event that George scripted in a rather casual way where Palpatine touched Anakin's forehead," the actor explained, citing the point when Palpatine knelt beside his badly burned apprentice on Mustafar. "I think that was really the only human moment we saw in the Emperor. Just a flash of sympathy and compassion for another human being. And sympathy and compassion are not ingredients of the Sith. It's not like he didn't have these feelings, just that they were irrelevant [to him]. There are people like that in the world today. It's not that they don't have a moral center, it just doesn't exist for them and their lives are run by the whole process of political manipulation and accruing power. And once ultimate power is not enough, the main motivating force is total greed, and nothing is ever enough, no circumstances are too awful to obtain those ends."

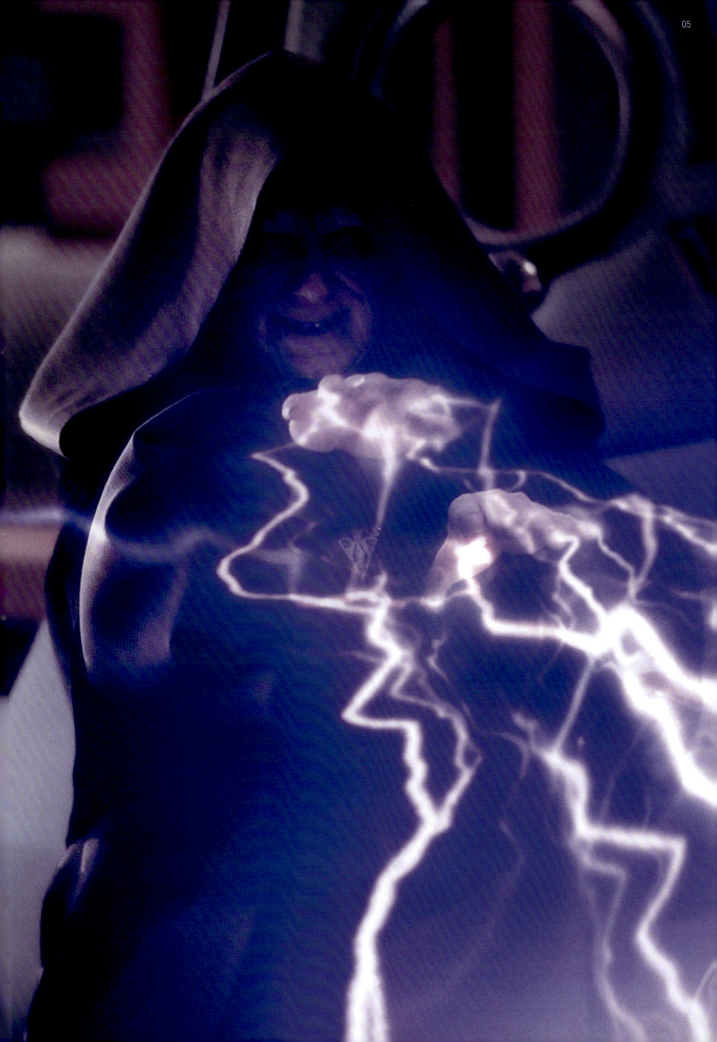

STAR WARS: REVENGE OF THE SITH SPECIAL
VOICE OF EVIL

VOICE OF EVIL
MATTHEW WOOD: GENERAL GRIEVOUS

General Grievous was not only a brilliant military strategist; the fiendish cyborg leader of the Separatist Droid Army was also a fearsome Jedi hunter with lightsaber skills that could defeat even the best the Order had to offer. Beneath his skeletal droid body, fearsome yellow eyes, gut-sack, and hacking cough were the only evidence that this ruthless creature had once been flesh and blood.

In the fall of 2002, George Lucas, producer Rick McCallum, concept artists, and key production members met each Friday to review the latest designs for *Revenge of the Sith*. On November 22, Lucas told the assembly that the movie's villain could be a Separatist droid general. "I won't limit it at this point to a droid. It could be an alien of some kind. I'm not sure if I want him to be human. It's the Darth Maul. It's the Jango Fett. Darth Vader," he's recorded explaining in *The Making of Return of the Sith*. He told the artists the villain was not a Sith, should be able to do dialogue scenes, and had to be iconic.

And so General Grievous, the Supreme Commander of the Separatist Droid Army, was born. Two weeks after Lucas' instruction to design the foe, concept artist Warren Fu presented illustrations for the character that caught the director's eye. Fellow concept artist Ian McCaig had advised them to think of their worst nightmares, and Fu imagined a scary masked enemy. His designs became the foundation for the fearsome cyborg who would stalk across the big screen in the final *Star Wars* prequel.

A combination of robotic technology with an organic base, General Grievous' voice was grating and loud, part mechanical and part biological. That voice was provided by Matthew Wood, supervising sound editor and sound designer at Skywalker Sound, and it came to be rather late in the process. "My first look at what a fully rendered Grievous was going to look like was actually in *Star Wars Insider*," Wood revealed. "It was on the cover, and I remember thinking, 'Whoa, that's cool. Who's gonna voice that?' Because the character had no mouth, we could wait a certain amount of time before Industrial Light & Magic needed our final voice-overs."

Busy working on audio effects for *Revenge of the Sith*, Wood knew that Lucas wanted the voice to sound as if it was synthesized through the circuitry of a voice box, with computerized, cybernetic qualities, and he and co-sound editor Christopher Scarabosio developed a distinctive resonance for Grievous. "We ran it through some processing, including ring modulation, to give it that synthesized timbre. We put every audition we got through that same process, as an egalitarian method for every actor's performance. I would play those for George to get his feedback on what things he did or didn't like. And I had the ability to sit in on all those auditions and also process them," Wood explained.

66 | STAR WARS: REVENGE OF THE SITH

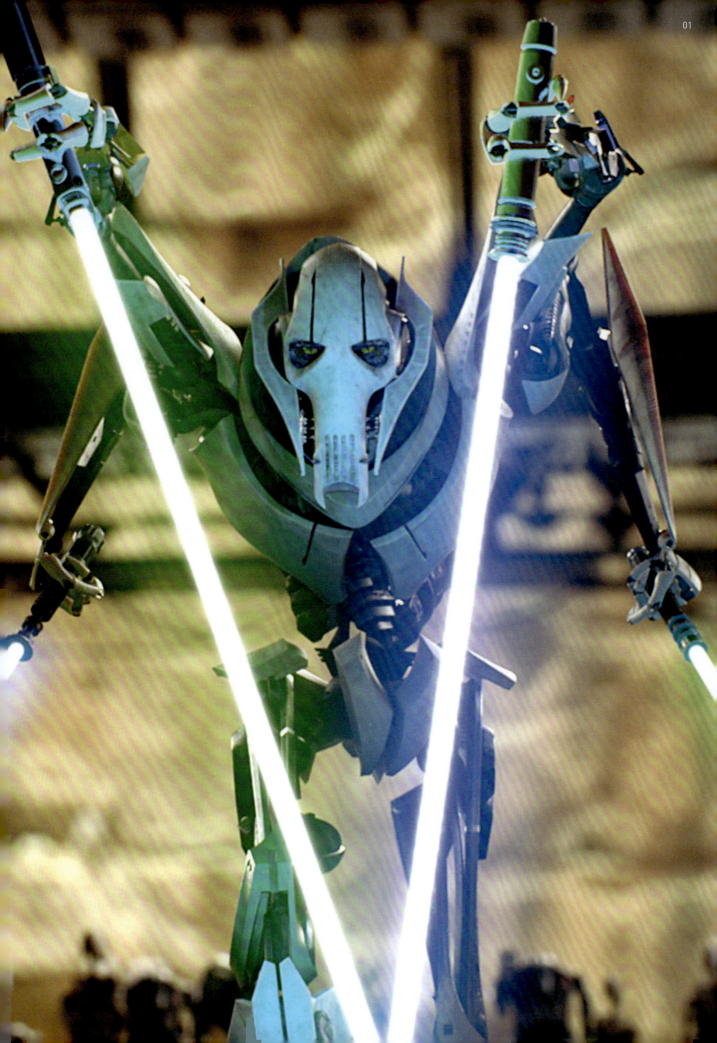

STAR WARS: REVENGE OF THE SITH SPECIAL
VOICE OF EVIL

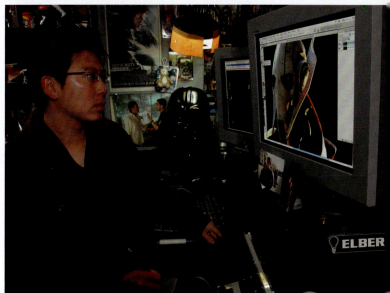

01 Previous page: General Grievous, voiced by Matthew Wood.

02 Concept artist Warren Fu came up with the iconic design for the Separatist general.

03 Obi-Wan Kenobi (Ewan McGregor) and General Grievous trading blows on Utapau.

04 Lead viewpainter Elbert Yen working on General Grievous' CG textures.

Having that perspective put Wood in a unique position. McCallum was getting nervous because they needed to cast the role of Grievous and time was running out, so Scarabosio encouraged Wood to audition. Wood, a trained actor, had contributed voice performances in *Star Wars* productions previously, so he anonymously submitted his file to Lucas with the other auditions. He approached Grievous with a gruff voice, something to convey the character's militaristic sense. And he also added a little old-school villain style, in the vein of 1930s horror movie actor Bela Lugosi. Wood recalled, "I'd coincidentally come back from visiting a friend in Prague, so it was fresh in my mind and that's what I went with: yelling in a classic villain voice with an Eastern European accent. As that hit the processor, I could hear there was this nice gravelly quality. Then I got the surprising call that George had picked my audition."

Wood's performance of General Grievous' biting metallic voice cut through the Battle of Coruscant in *Revenge of the Sith*'s opening scenes, as Anakin Skywalker (Hayden Christensen) and Obi-Wan Kenobi (Ewan McGregor) confronted the general after his kidnapping of Supreme Chancellor Palpatine. As it turns out, McGregor never knew who voiced Grievous until some years after the movie's release. Grievous battled with Kenobi more than once in the movie, and during filming McGregor was most often sparring with stunt double Kyle Rowling, who stood in for the CG cyborg, with Grievous' lines being read from off-camera. "I worked with Ewan in my sound capacity on all the prequels," Wood said. "I'd record him all the time for the post-production dialogue recording we had to do. It wasn't until I worked with him years later, when I brought him in to do a whispery voice for *Star Wars: The Force Awakens*, that I actually got to tell him, 'Hey, did you know what ended up happening with that voice? It was me.' And he was like, 'No way!'"

After Dooku's death, Grievous took over his position and moved the Separatist

STAR WARS: REVENGE OF THE SITH SPECIAL

VOICE OF EVIL

05

Council from Utapau to Mustafar at Darth Sidious' behest. The over-confident cyborg engaged with Kenobi for what would be the final time, as the duel ended with Grievous' death. To his last, Grievous barked out orders and taunts punctuated by a phlegmy cough. Lucas wanted Grievous to have breathing troubles because he was essentially a testing ground for the technology that would eventually create Darth Vader. By luck, both Wood and Lucas were in a state to provide the required rattles and hacks.

"For a lot of those lines, I really had to use my diaphragm big time and yell this guttural performance," Wood recalled. "I would run out of breath and cough, and George himself had a really bad cough that day. I remember telling Chris Scarabosio to keep the tape rolling, because George would come up to direct me and he would start coughing. We captured a lot of George's really bad coughs from the day and ended up rolling some of them into Grievous' performance."

Wood thinks of Grievous' voice as a two-part composition: the dramatic element and the processing layer. "I pitched him down about a semi-tone to give him that lower pitch register, and in a way where his voice had an artifacting quality to it where it doesn't sound perfect," he explained. "I was going for imperfection, so when he was yelling, I wanted to make it almost like he was so angry that his vocal processor was unable to translate his emotion into voice perfectly."

Wood had to perform a hyper-enunciated yell in order to get Grievous' words and emotion across through the gravelly, scratchy qualities in his voice. The ring-modulation and delay Wood applied was not unlike the standard procedure he used for droid processing, but Grievous got a little something extra. "It was a mix and match of a few different things, because George wanted to communicate that Grievous had a biological component to illustrate that he had a weakness," said Wood. "The cough was supposed to illustrate that, too. It's such an odd and creepy character. It's a part I've really loved and respected all these years."

05 General Grievous reveals his ability to fight using four lightsabers.

STAR WARS: REVENGE OF THE SITH | 69

ORDER 66
THE HAMMER FALLS

The Jedi paid a terrible price for the Clone Wars. With its greatest warriors scattered on many different fronts and cut off from the Temple as the conflict reached its final phase, they found themselves in the firing line of their own clone troopers when Palpatine initiated Order 66. *Star Wars Insider* chronicled the filming of the death scenes of several prominent Jedi.

he first casualty of Order 66 filmed at Fox Studios, Australia was Plo Koon. Matt Sloan, who worked behind the scenes as a droid-unit mechanic, donned the robes of the Jedi Master on August 8, 2003. In addition to his skills with radio-controlled astromechs, Sloan made a fine pilot as he took the control yoke of the Jedi starfighter prop, mounted on a rig on Stage 4.

The same prop, which also doubled for Anakin Skywalker and Obi-Wan Kenobi's starfighters at the start of the movie, was equipped with a detachable pod to facilitate the shooting of close-ups, and was secured to a manually operated gimbal so stagehands could rock and tilt it to simulate turbulence. Lights mounted to a curved monorail track positioned above the cockpit were triggered at director George Lucas' cue to arc over the rear of the set and flash on and off, simulating the blasts of explosions erupting all around as the ship banked and turned.

However, Plo Koon had to contend with more than turbulence when he came under fire from his own clone trooper wingmen. Two pyrotechnic charges were set in the rear of the cockpit and when Lucas shouted, "Now!" they ignited with bright flashes. Sloan lunged forwards amid showers of sparks, and thus Plo's end was captured on the first take. Spectators, gathered around the set, cheered and toasted with champagne when it was over. They weren't celebrating the Jedi's demise, but the fact that the completion of the shot marked the halfway point of principle photography.

Ki-Adi-Mundi was the only other Jedi to fall victim to Order 66 during principal photography, with only two more days of filming left to go, and the final shot on the call sheet on September 15. Actor Silas Carson performed his character's death alone against a green-screen set on Stage 3. Industrial Light & Magic would add in the ash-ridden planet Mygeeto, and the accompanying clone troops, much later. Lucas' direction was simple: "You turn and look at the clones. They pull out their guns and blam, blam, blam!"

During post-production, Amy Allen reprised her role as Ayla Secura on May 6, 2004. The blue-skinned Twi'lek Jedi worked alone on a green-screen stage, leading imaginary troops and prowling through a jungle that didn't exist yet, except as animatics. As with other planets, Felucia was so unearthly that it would have to be realized at a later date, using ILM's visual effects. A miniature four-by-four-foot tabletop version of the Felucia landscape was built by ILM for reference. Carefully-lit photography of this model served as a guide for the final computer renderings to ground the exotic planet with elements of physical reality.

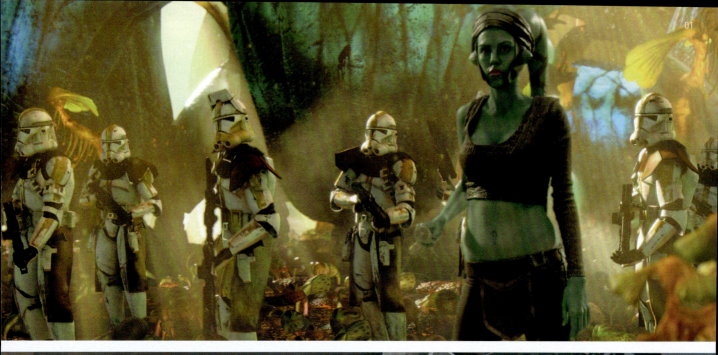

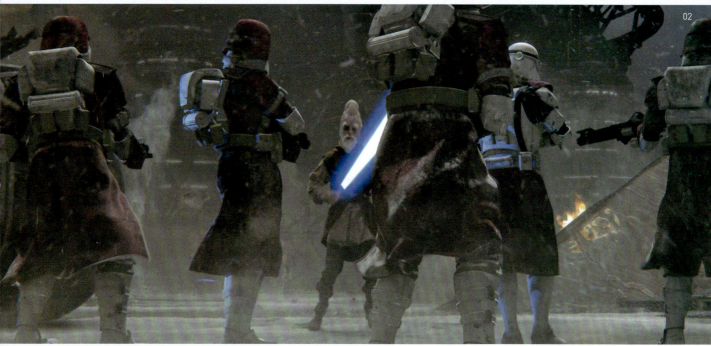

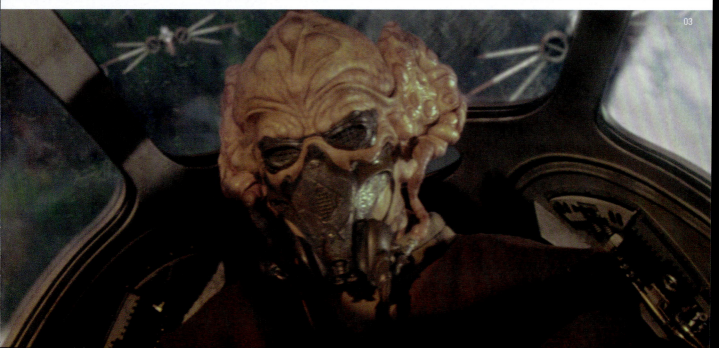

04

01-03 Previous page: Jedi Masters Ayla Secura (Amy Allen), Ki-Adi-Mundi (Silas Carson) and Plo Koon (Matt Sloan).

04 Kit Fisto was no match for Palpatine, a secret Sith Lord.

05 A new Kit Fisto mask was made for stunt performer Ben Cooke, who played the role in *Revenge of the Sith*.

06 Prosthetic makeup technicians Katherine Brown and Sophie Fleming applying the Kit Fisto mask to Ben Cooke.

07 ILM's Lauren Vogt (middle) adjusting actor Tux Akindoyeni's makeup.

08 Stass Allie (Nina Fallon) flying alongside a clone trooper, moments before Order 66.

09 Visual effects supervisor John Knoll directed Stass Allie's death during post-production.

10 ILM's reference model of the Felicia landscape.

As Jedi Knights Agen Kolar and Saesee Tiin would both appear in close-ups for their grim final moments, original actors Tux Akindoyeni (Kolar) and Kenji Oates (Tiin) were called back. Oates endured a lengthy makeup session for a shot that would take less than thirty seconds to film. Lucas directed the scene, closely comparing what had been shot in Sydney during principal photography and what was required for the insert. "Be sure to twist your body this way," he instructed Oates. "Swing the lightsaber back that way and shout out as you go down. Don't be afraid to scream." Oates' fake alien teeth and the blurring action made a nuanced performance difficult, but he managed a few strangled "aghs!" and a "gah!" if not an ear-piercing wail.

The last Jedi to meet her end for *Revenge of the Sith* was Stass Allie, whose execution was shot very late in post-production under the direction of ILM's John Knoll. On this occasion, the Jedi was portrayed by alien and visual effects coordinator Nina Fallon, no less than the third performer to fill Allie's long boots, the Jedi having previously been played by Lily Nyamwasa and Tace Bayliss. If you factor in that Stass was essentially a recast of Adi Gallia (Allie's cousin in *Star Wars* lore), then that number jumps up to four to account for Gin Clarke, who portrayed Gallia in *The Phantom Menace*. This was nothing new. There are at least three Plo Koons, four Saesee Tinns, three Luminara Undulis, three Shaak Tis, and four Kit Fistos scattered throughout the prequel trilogy, if you know where to look.

05

06

07

72 | STAR WARS: REVENGE OF THE SITH

STAR WARS: REVENGE OF THE SITH SPECIAL

ORDER 66: THE HAMMER FALLS

09 Once again, the action was shot on an all-green stage. A green wooden sawhorse with handlebars stood in for Allie's speeder bike, providing the correct ergonomic structure for Fallon to adopt the attentive rider's position. Knoll's simple direction was: "There's a big battle on this planet, but it's over for now, so, you're flying around, still aware of potential trouble. Yeah, that's it." Fallon followed orders, but her Jedi robes did not. Despite the presence of a wind machine, the gusts weren't big enough to effectively billow her cloak out. The solution: the stage crew brought in a bigger fan.

10 The desert plains of Saleucami, marked with spindly palm trees and rocks, were a late addition to the planetary lineup. Their design was originally developed for additional scenes to take place on Felucia that were never filmed, including one in which Stass Allie was to split off on her speeder bike from Secura's group. However, in order to inject more planetary diversity during the Order 66 sequence, the locations of both Jedi's deaths were instead broken up onto different worlds.

STAR WARS: REVENGE OF THE SITH | 73

11

12

11 Palpatine slays Agen Kolar as Saesee Tiin prepares to strike back.

12 Creature shop supervisor Colin Ware preparing to airbrush makeup to actor Kenji Oates (Saesee Tiin).

13 Continuity photos of Eeth Koth, played by Hassani Shappi (left) in *The Phantom Menace*. New character Agen Kolar was created after Tux Akindoyeni (right) appeared as Koth during the Geonosis battle scenes in *Attack of the Clone*s.

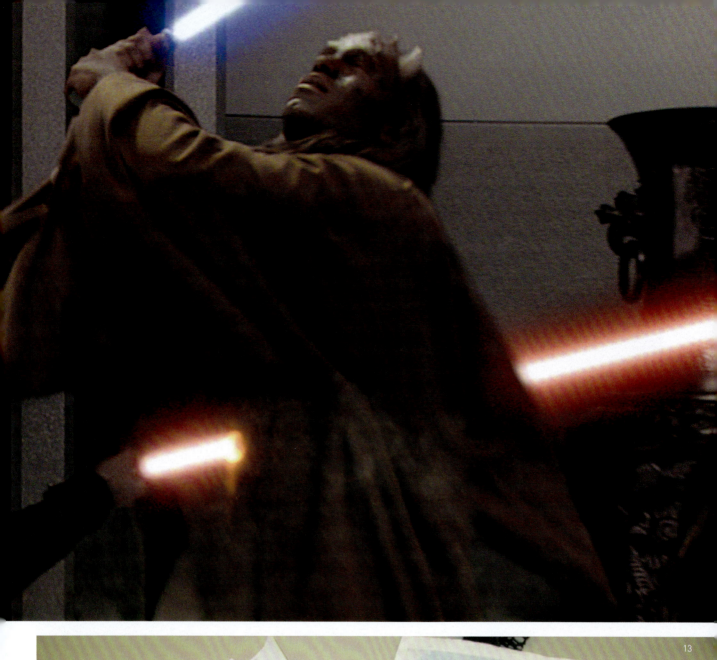
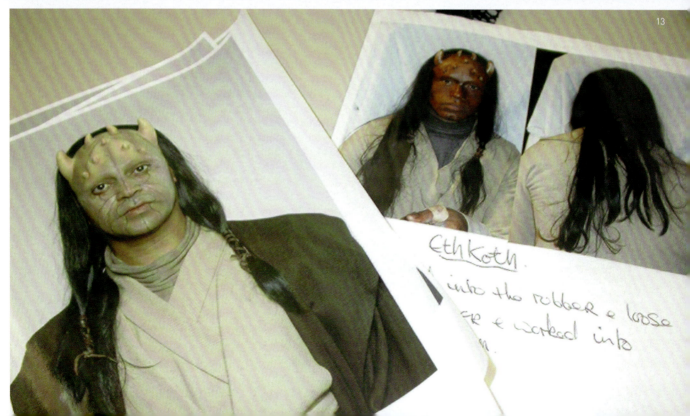

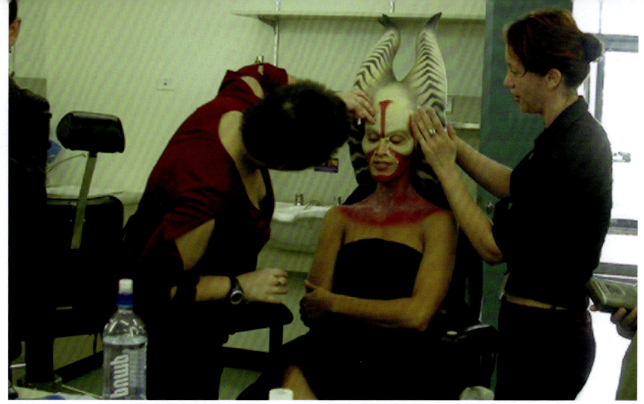

14

14 Orli Shoshan underwent a lengthy makeup session to portray Shaak Ti.

15 Shaak Ti's second shot at a big on-screen death was filmed but again didn't make the final cut.

The Cruel Fate Of Shaak Ti

While numerous Jedi generals were slain by blaster fire from their once-loyal clone troopers, a greater indignity was reserved for one particular member of the Order: getting cut from the film entirely.

As the shooting script was coming together, department heads were kept apprised of the storyline as it affected them. They had already set up shop in Sydney and the pressure was on. All manner of tests—makeup, camera, costumes, et al—were well underway in May 2003, so they could be as prepared as possible for when actual production began. A printed chart of headshots labeled "Episode III Jedi" was tacked to the wall of both the Hair and Makeup department and the Creature Shop. Sixteen Jedi were featured on the chart, not all of whom made the final cut.

Shaak Ti has the dubious distinction of being cut from the film not once, but twice. Originally, she would have been referenced in a line of dialogue during the opening space battle, with the Jedi having been at Supreme Chancellor Palpatine's side when he was kidnapped by General Grievous. This would have led to a scene introducing Grievous as he stabbed Shaak Ti through the heart with her own lightsaber, right in front of Anakin and Obi-Wan.

The scene was shot with actor Orli Shoshan playing the Jedi, and Duncan Young—the offscreen dialogue reader—standing in as Grievous, balanced on an apple box to provide suitable eyelines for the other performers. However, the opening sequence aboard the cruiser was running too long in the edit, taking too much time to reach the meat of the story, so Lucas excised such serial-type high jinks. Shaak Ti was a victim of those cuts, and all reference to her at the start of the film was removed, sparing her a grisly death in the process.

"It was something I thought was great," said concept artist Ian McCaig at the time. He, along with Derek Thompson, had helped develop the sequence in pre-production through storyboards. "It was a way of introducing Grievous the way Darth Vader was introduced to us [in *A New Hope*] when he strangles that rebel officer. You knew he was a bad guy."

There was something about the image of Shaak Ti convulsing as a lightsaber speared her heart that stuck with Lucas, and she would face another executioner in front of cameras a few months later. During the pick-up shots at Shepperton Studios in London, Shoshan was scheduled for a single scene of shooting, and she traveled from Australia to London to brave the makeup process once again. The new scene was eerily similar to the one previously cut, but instead of sitting disconsolately on the floor of General Grievous' starship, the *Invisible Hand*, Shaak Ti sat on one of the thick disc-like ottomans that Jedi had in their private quarters. With film noir shadows cast across her by a slatted blind, a hooded Hayden Christensen as Darth Vader stepped into the frame. "What is it, Skywalker?" Shaak Ti asked. There was no answer other than a stab in the back.

Most of the morning of September 3, 2004— the last day of a very busy two weeks-worth of shooting—was dedicated to Shaak Ti's demise, but, for all that effort, it was cut from the movie. A scene of her in the Temple did make it into the novelization, however.

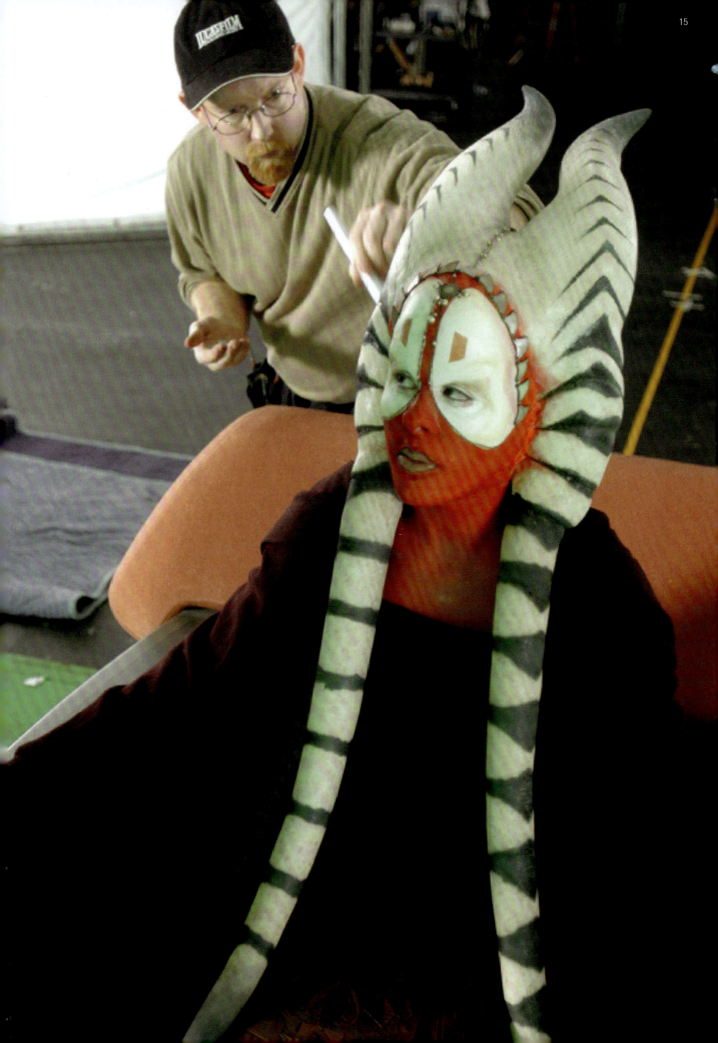

A MUSICAL JOURNEY

As had become a tradition with *Star Wars* movies, following the rolling drums and fanfare of the 20th Century Fox and Lucasfilm logos, fans would brace themselves for the first triumphant blast of brass that heralded the opening of *Revenge of the Sith*. However, the famous "Main Title" theme was not the first piece of music to be recorded at the Episode III scoring sessions.

Composer John Williams wrote more than 40 distinct cues for the Episode III score, which were performed over the span of a few days with the London Symphony Orchestra at Abbey Road Studios in London, in February 2005. Just as during principal photography, the scoring of the movie wouldn't follow the same chronological sequence as its plot. In fact, the first piece of music recorded for *Sith* came from some six reels into the story, titled "Padmé's Visit," a musical cue that accompanied a tense and dramatic encounter between Anakin Skywalker and Padmé Amidala. There's a sense of desperation behind it, of time ticking away. Anakin's troubled nature is signaled by the creeping approach of the "Imperial March," Darth Vader's theme from *The Empire Strikes Back*. The deep bass tones that lurk behind the love theme color the drama.

Astonishingly, prior to the sessions, the 110-musician strong London Symphony Orchestra had not seen Williams' score, let alone any footage from the movie. They played each cue through once before recording it—left to imagine just what events might be transpiring in the film itself, with Williams offering words of guidance or necessary modifications—before tapes rolled.

The next cue on the schedule hailed from the early moments of the film, and the first lightsaber duel in a movie packed with many—the three-way rematch that saw Anakin and Obi-Wan Kenobi squaring off against Count Dooku. Percussive music accented with cymbal hits underscores the lightsaber fight, but it isn't particularly timed to each hit—impractical given the intensity of the sound design that would accompany the action. An angry roll of timpani drums accompanies the fight's denouement, silencing the orchestra in its wake. Then tentative strings come in, exploring the uncomfortable silence that follows.

"Can the clicks be louder?" Williams asked the engineer, Sean Murphy, in the control room. "They sound a bit woolly."

The assembled musicians wore earpieces during the sessions, through which they could hear a click track—a series of regular clicks that helped them keep in time. Seated in the control room, carefully listening to the orchestra as they recorded, Murphy complied. Part of his role was to note on any irregularities in the music, citing parts that would need to be revisited. After each take, Williams would head into the control room, along with the principal musicians, to hear what the microphones had captured. Together, Murphy and Williams gauged each performance and determined which needed retakes. Rather than wear down the orchestra by recording entire cues again, they often targeted specific trouble spots, prompting the orchestra to replay certain sections that would later be edited into the surrounding music.

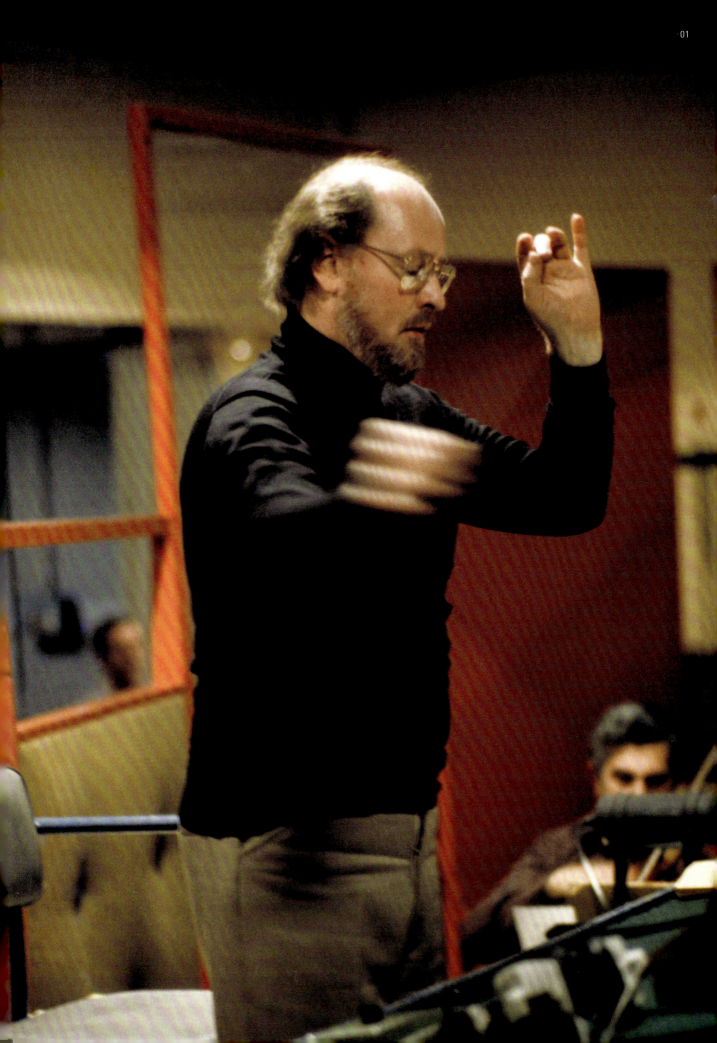

STAR WARS: REVENGE OF THE SITH SPECIAL

A MUSICAL JOURNEY

01 Previous page: Composer John Williams conducting the London Symphony Orchestra during scoring for *Star Wars: A New Hope*.

02 Cue 6M9 "Revenge of the Sith" added orchestral flair to Obi-Wan Kenobi's duel with Anakin Skywalker.

03 Williams' *Star Wars* career is celebrated in the 2024 Disney+ documentary, *Music by John Williams*.

04 Anakin (Hayden Christensen) learns the truth about who Supreme Chancellor Palpatine (Ian McDiarmid) really is.

The next selection for the day was "Palpatine's Seduction," scoring a conversation between Anakin and Palpatine within the supreme chancellor's office. Even in the heavily soundproofed confines of the control room, the low vibrations could be felt. A strong connection stirs between Anakin and Palpatine as voiced by the strings, while a bass drum is responsible for the tremors.

"I love the dark stuff," noted the attending director George Lucas, who clearly relished the moody tones provided throughout Williams' score.

Next up was "Heroes Collide," the beginning of the much-anticipated duel between Kenobi and Skywalker. This new theme, carried mostly by the brass section, follows the two Jedi as their duel takes them from an exterior landing platform to the inside of an industrial facility. The music alternates between fast punctuation and sweeping strokes, not unlike the lightsaber duel itself. Murphy noted that the sound quality of the loud percussion was affecting the rest of the orchestra, so Williams conducted the next take without the percussion. As it turned out, even the huge Abbey Road stage was too small to contain the powerful drums. They would be recorded later under different circumstances.

Lucas pointed out that the fight seemed to be lacking an expected ingredient, "The Duel of the Fates" cue from *The Phantom Menace*. "That comes later in the big duel," Williams reminded him.

While only four pieces were slated for that day's recordings, the orchestra had time to perform more cues. "Yoda's Fault" is a very brief piece that underscores a specific action, less than a minute in length, while "Revisiting Padmé" covers the reunion of the Skywalker lovers. It contains the familiar love theme from Episode II but introduces an interesting juxtaposition in tone. An undercurrent of dark uncertainty.

STAR WARS: REVENGE OF THE SITH SPECIAL

A MUSICAL JOURNEY

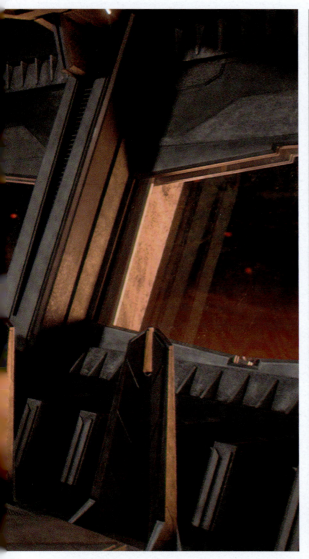

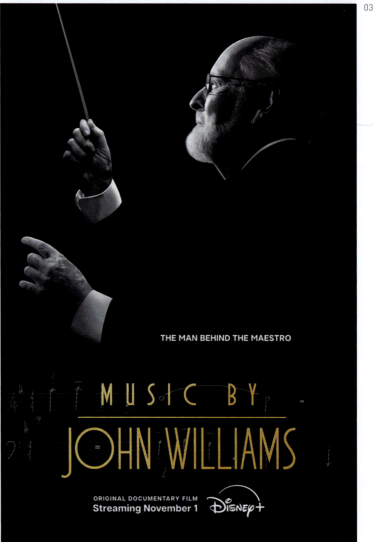

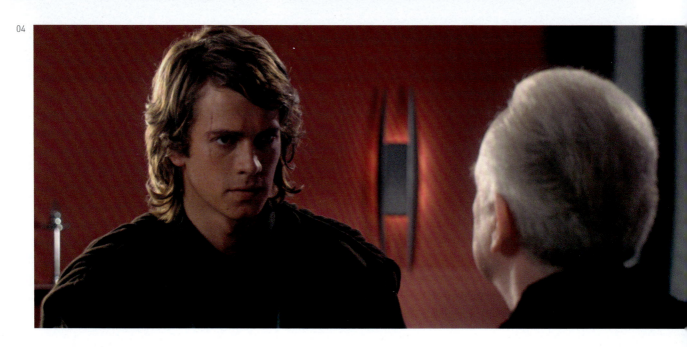

STAR WARS: REVENGE OF THE SITH SPECIAL
A MUSICAL JOURNEY

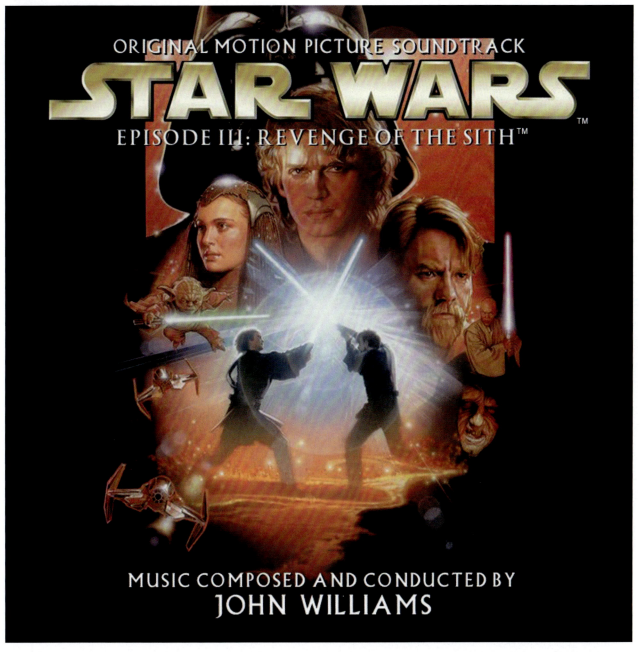

05 The cover of the *Revenge of the Sith* soundtrack.

06 The love theme from *Attack of the Clones* was given an undercurrent of dark uncertainty for *Revenge of the Sith*.

07 Recording of the *Sith* score at London's Abbey Road Studios.

Recording Revenge

With each *Star Wars* soundtrack, Williams selected a particular composition to stand apart, its start or end reworked to be used as a standalone musical piece to promote the movie. For Episode III, a dramatic cue from the 6th reel would be the one to receive special attention. Cue 6M9, appropriately named "Revenge of the Sith," appears during the thick of the duel between Kenobi and Skywalker. The first half of the second day of scoring sessions consisted of capturing this piece for inclusion both in the film and as a modified version for the soundtrack release. Additional heavy percussion as well as the emotional sweep provided by a choir were recorded later.

As with most of the combat and action cues, the timing and tempo were carefully controlled by the click track piped into the musician's earpieces. "We made it through the first three *Star Wars* without click tracks, but we really need to use those clicks in this," observed Williams. When the principal musicians crowded into the control room to listen to the take—and for the first time see the footage that had been playing on a screen behind them—they gasped at the right moment, just as the composer and director had intended.

"I can't wait to hear the chorus," George Lucas said. "It has a tendency to smooth things out and add a lot of emotion."

"Even though it's large and

STAR WARS: REVENGE OF THE SITH SPECIAL

A MUSICAL JOURNEY

somewhat military in its sound, find a way to add some nobility to it," Williams advised the orchestra before another take was recorded.

For the first cue of the next day, there was perhaps more familiarity with the music the orchestra would be playing. "Good morning, people," Williams announced to the assembled musicians. "We'll start with 7M8, the end credits."

As all *Star Wars* fans know, the end credit sequence follows a very specific structure. With the iris out of the last frame of the film, a triple attack of brassy fanfare kicks into the main title theme, an up-tempo rendition of the *Star Wars* theme. With *Revenge of the Sith* serving double duty as a finale to the entire saga, the end credits would be slightly different this time around, containing a major piece of music that otherwise had no place in the prequels.

After the fanfare of the main theme dies down, the glide of a harp segues into "Princess Leia's theme," now indelibly associated with the peacefulness of Alderaan, one of the final worlds seen in Episode III. It is perhaps the most passionate and emotional cue in the entire *Star Wars* saga, and the recording ended with rousing applause and tears of appreciation from the orchestra.

"It will be another twenty-five years before we do this again," joked Williams.

STAR WARS: REVENGE OF THE SITH | 83

STAR WARS: REVENGE OF THE SITH SPECIAL

SITH UNSEEN

SITH UNSEEN
BEYOND THE MOVIE

Collectibles, merchandise, and all kinds of licensed products have been a part of *Star Wars* since the very beginning, and appeal to both hardcore fans and collectors alike. But often these supplements to the main feature films offer more than simply tie-in entertainment. For *Star Wars: Revenge of the Sith*, novels, games, and comics expanded beyond the confines of its onscreen story.

I n an age where intricately planned cinematic universes create a web of narrative links between movies and their spin-offs, modern-genre fans have become accustomed to seeing the latest blockbusters arrive with an abundance of tie-in materials, in the form of videogames, novels, comics, and more. These supplementary sources often divulge details and subplots that relate to the feature's central story, offering fans a more immersive experience exploring the characters and events concerned, beyond the confines of the movie itself.

While this approach is now commonplace—and has been a core element of Lucasfilm's storytelling since 2014—the company pioneered the use of a well-focused, multimedia push when *Star Wars: Revenge of the Sith* was released on May 19, 2005. Prior to that date, expectant fans could already play *Star Wars*: Republic Commando to get a sneak peek of General Grievous and the buildup to the Battle of Kashyyyk. Once the film hit theaters, fans who wondered about Obi-Wan Kenobi's cryptic line concerning "that business on Cato Neimoidia" had the chance to read James Luceno's *Labyrinth of Evil* and discover the story behind it. Anyone who wanted to learn about the film's aftermath need only turn to Luceno's follow-up novel, *Dark Lord: The Rise of Darth Vader*. [Ed. note: Both of which are now considered part of the Legends Series of books.]

The connections presented in these off-screen offerings alluded to *Revenge of the Sith* in various ways, from referencing unseen characters to describing the events that immediately preceded the movie's opening crawl. While these stories have since been superseded by new tales from Marvel, Del Rey, and others, the plots of the most prominent licensed product from 2005 offer a fascinating window on efforts at the time to create a cohesive narrative across different media.

84 | STAR WARS: REVENGE OF THE SITH

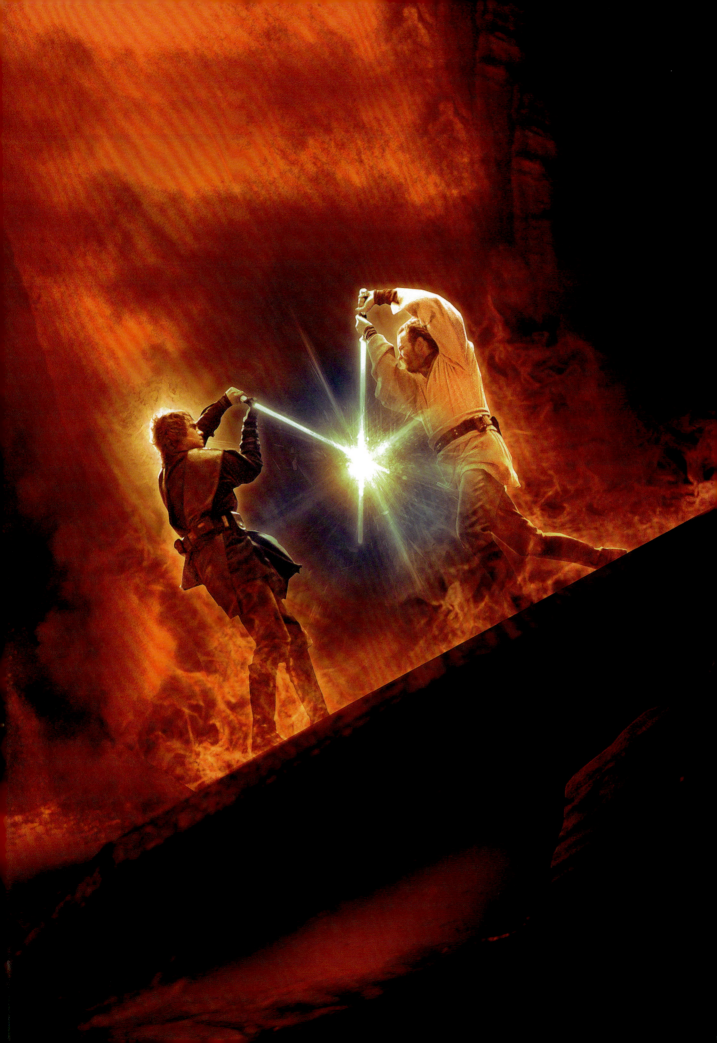

STAR WARS: REVENGE OF THE SITH SPECIAL

SITH UNSEEN

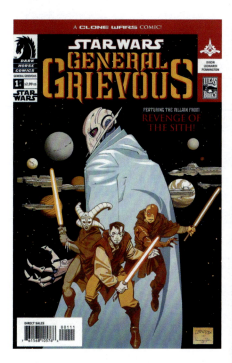

Star Wars: General Grievous (Legends)

AUTHOR: Chuck Dixon
PENCILS: Rick Leonardi
INKS: Mark Pen
RELEASE DATE: March to August 2005
PUBLISHER: Dark Horse Comics

Set a year prior to the events of *Revenge of the Sith*, the four-issue *General Grievous* comic emphasizes the Separatist leader's status as a murderous war criminal who poses an imminent threat to the Jedi. Combined with Count Dooku's training, Grievous' metallic physique and fiendish demeanor generate a ruthless killing machine, leading three Jedi to become so concerned that they renounce their membership of the Order to track the General down and assassinate him.

In the meantime, Grievous continues to ravage the Republic by slaughtering a Mon Calamari starship's crew, ordering another Jedi's execution, capturing several Padawans, and leading a genocidal invasion that wipes out the majority of Ugnaughts living on their home planet. The General devises an even more diabolical fate for the Padawans: he envisions replacing much of their anatomy with droid exoskeletons designed to harness

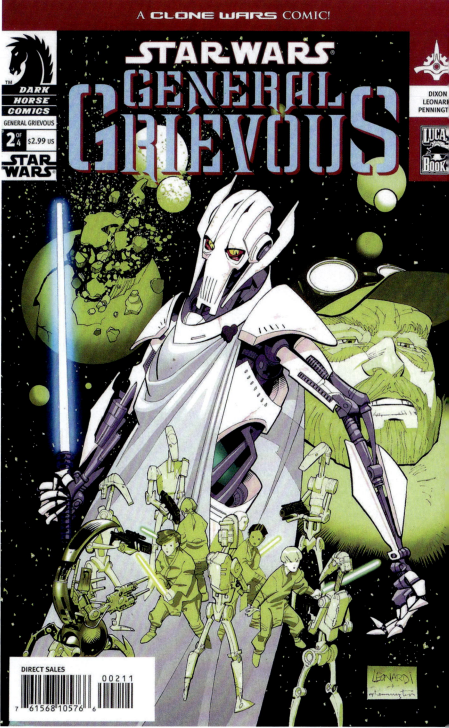

their Force talents for evil. When the Padawans escape their cell, Grievous quickly grows tired of the chase and prepares to put them to death. The rogue Jedi catch up with Grievous in the nick of time and prioritize saving the Padawans over eliminating their target. Two of the three would-be saviors even give their lives fighting Grievous, to buy enough time for the children to retreat off-world.

The comic establishes General Grievous as the imposing villain we see in *Revenge of the Sith*, and paints him as a ruthless beast in an effective effort to showcase why the galaxy fears the former Kaleesh warlord so much.

STAR WARS: REVENGE OF THE SITH SPECIAL

SITH UNSEEN

Labyrinth Of Evil
(Legends)

AUTHOR: James Luceno
RELEASE DATE: January 25, 2005
PUBLISHER: Del Rey

While *Star Wars*: Republic Commando deals with matters from a previously unknown clone trooper's perspective, *Labyrinth of Evil* follows the pre-*Revenge of the Sith* actions undertaken by major players Anakin Skywalker, Obi-Wan Kenobi, General Grievous, Count Dooku, Yoda, Mace Windu, and Darth Sidious.

The novel contains many tethers to the final episode in the prequel trilogy, yet takes time to create some interesting adventures of its own. Commander Cody, who would eventually betray Obi-Wan on Utapau, appears during Skywalker and Kenobi's attempt to capture Nute Gunray on Cato Neimoidia. We learn that Asajj Ventress gave Skywalker the scar on his face, and are introduced to the Jedi initiative to give the clones names and treat them with compassion.

Another oft-quoted slice of *Revenge of the Sith* dialogue—when Kenobi denies requiring Skywalker's help during "that business on Cato Neimoidia"—receives its own explanation here, too. Skywalker did protect Kenobi from a battle droid, but the statement most likely refers to a dire situation when the two Jedi found themselves separated. After losing his rebreather, Kenobi faces down dozens of battle droids while in a semi-drugged state. Skywalker rushes to save his master, only to discover that Kenobi has managed to defeat his mechanical foes despite his hallucinations. The notion of whether or not Skywalker saved his master soon becomes a matter of jovial ribbing between the two friends.

Elsewhere, Count Dooku privately muses to himself about Grievous' descent from fully organic being to technological hybrid. The novel explains that Dooku and Sidious masterminded the shuttle accident that left Grievous' body broken, forcing the General to agree to cybernetic augmentation. During the surgical process in Geonosis' depths, the two Sith order the Geonosians to manipulate the General's mind to make him believe he has always been ruthless. The alterations drive Grievous to genocide, massacring twenty seven Jedi and more than 10,000 civilians while invading Belderone.

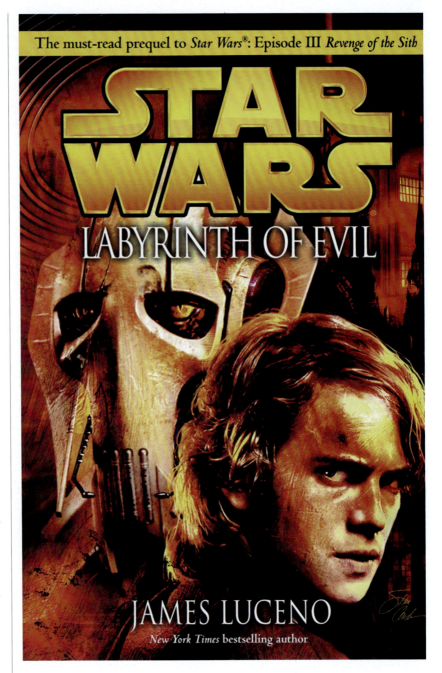

Then, Supreme Chancellor Palpatine delivers an address to the Senate about advancing into the Outer Rim, which lines up precisely with Kenobi's briefing in the movie regarding the sieges in that region. Palpatine highlights Mygeeto, Saleucami, and Felucia as key targets, and these three planets each make an appearance during Order 66's notorious Jedi execution sequence.

The novel also references Kenobi and Skywalker's lengthy service in the Outer Rim, on a secretive mission to hunt down Darth Sidious. The duo's deployment fits well with Skywalker and Padmé Amidala's emotional reunion after the Battle of Coruscant, as captured in the movie.

Labyrinth of Evil's final chapters chronicle the Separatists' surprise attack on Coruscant and Grievous' capture of Palpatine. The novel completes its tale with Skywalker and Kenobi readying themselves to jump to the Republic's capital and reinforce the fleet. The book was later packaged alongside the movie's novelization and *Dark Lord: The Rise of Darth Vader* as *The Dark Lord Trilogy*.

STAR WARS: REVENGE OF THE SITH SPECIAL

SITH UNSEEN

Star Wars: Republic Commando

RELEASE DATE: February 28, 2005
PUBLISHER: LucasArts

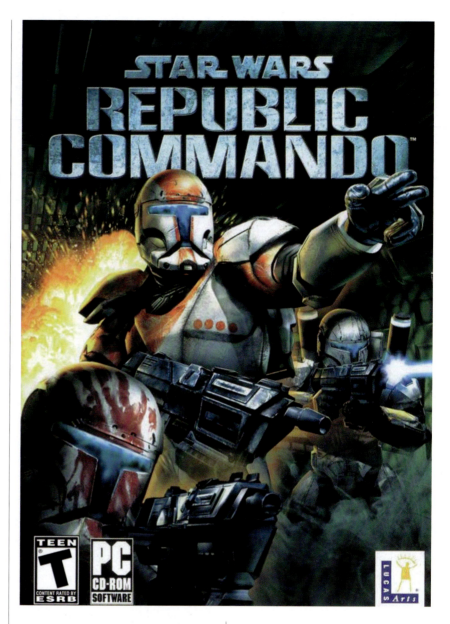

In this first-person videogame, players take on the role of RC-01/138, a clone commanding the elite unit Delta Squad. Nicknamed 'Boss,' you lead a team of three troopers into warzones strewn across the *Star Wars* galaxy.

The game's storyline follows Boss from the conflict's opening salvo at the First Battle of Geonosis, as seen in *Star Wars: Attack of the Clones* (2002), with the player guiding Delta Squad in missions that span the duration of the war. Levels include investigating the seemingly derelict *Acclamator*-class assault ship *Prosecutor* to a recognizable engagement on the planet Kashyyyk.

Delta Squad's excursion to the Wookiee homeworld includes numerous links to *Revenge of the Sith*. Boss and his comrades arrive on Kashyyyk prior to the Battle of Coruscant, where they uncover General Grievous and the Separatists collaborating with Trandoshan slavers on a plan to enslave the local population. The Trandoshans have imprisoned Tarfful, the Wookiee chieftain who later works with Chewbacca to facilitate Master Yoda's escape after Order 66. Delta Squad successfully rescue Tarfful from his reptilian captors and, possessing the vital intelligence they've uncovered, Tarfful leaves the planet in order to deliver the data to Coruscant. Grievous escapes to his ship, the *Invisible Hand*, linking the game directly to the opening space battle of Episode III.

The Separatist presence on Kashyyyk in Republic Commando is what prompts Master Ki-Adi-Mundi's question to the Jedi Council in *Revenge of the Sith*:

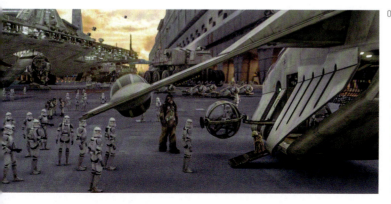

"What about the droid attack on the Wookiees?" In response, Yoda announces he will oversee the Republic's response to this invasion, and Tarfful can clearly be seen waiting when the Jedi Master

01

01 Yoda and Tarfful preparing to help the Wookiees defend their homeworld against a Separatist attack.

arrives at the troop staging area to prepare for departure. Back on Kashyyyk, Boss and Delta Squad operate against the Separatists in Tarfful's home city of Kachirho, contributing covering fire for the Republic's reinforcements.

The game concludes on a cliffhanger, with Delta Squad ordered to exfiltrate aboard a gunship and await further instructions. At that point, Yoda has arrived on the scene, ready to head up the Clone Army's war strategy. Republic Commando's final moments tease the upcoming Battle of Kashyyyk that would feature in *Revenge of the Sith*, setting the stage for the Separatists' offensive against the clone troopers and Wookiees who are establishing defensive positions on Kachirho's beaches.

STAR WARS: REVENGE OF THE SITH SPECIAL

SITH UNSEEN

Star Wars: Episode III Revenge Of The Sith

AUTHOR: Matthew Stover
RELEASE DATE: April 2, 2005
PUBLISHER: Del Rey

In 2005, Matthew Stover joined an exclusive club of authors including Alan Dean Foster, Donald F. Glut, James Conn, Terry Brooks, and R.A. Salvatore, who had penned a *Star Wars* movie novelization. "I think what I did was a little bit different from the common run of movie adaptations," he told *Star Wars Insider*. "Rather than trying to recreate the film in book form, I was trying to write it as though it were a novel the movie was being adapted from." Stover's novelization puts the reader inside different characters' heads, something literature can do but film, for all its visual power, cannot. The result, he hoped, "was a companion piece rather than a retelling, so people who saw the film first would still find some surprises in the novel."

The adaptation had an additional advantage in that the author was able to discuss the characters and story with George Lucas himself. "In many ways, he was much like any other *Star Wars* fan," Stover remembered, saying that Lucas was, "Excited talking about this stuff. He had so much story in his head, it was like everything he said would remind him of something else on the same subject."

The *Revenge of the Sith* novelization primarily relays the film's consequential scenes, but it also opens a previously unseen window into the thoughts and motivations that influenced notable actions. Anakin Skywalker's visions pertaining to Padmé's death during childbirth, his desire to protect her, and his anger over not being granted the rank of Jedi Master, are all well-documented onscreen, but the novelization lends further insight into the young man's frustration relating to his status on the Council. He knows the Jedi Temple contains holocrons filled with knowledge from generations of Jedi, but protocol states that only Jedi Masters retain access to those resources. Anakin initially plans to research other Jedi who experienced prophecies and whether the foreseen events could be prevented, but his focus shifts when Palpatine tells him about Darth Plagueis' ability to save people from death. In Skywalker's mind, he

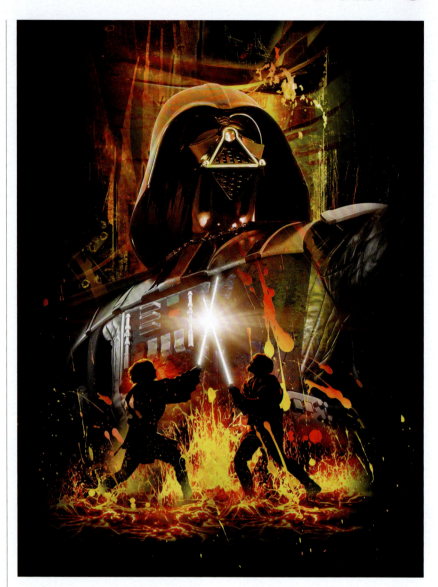

needs to become a master so that he has a chance to dig through the Archives, learn as much as possible about Plagueis, and save Padmé.

Just as *Labyrinth of Evil* expounds on its source material, this novelization offers additional insight into familiar scenes. For instance, while the war rages, Palpatine disturbs his critics by installing Republic governors accompanied by clone units to many planets. Allegedly sent to help local officials, these forces surely act as a foothold for the Imperial government once the Empire replaces the Republic.

Equally, on his way to altering the message being broadcast by the Jedi Temple's beacon, the book also reveals Kenobi's humorous ruse to dispatch the troopers guarding the building. He poses as a hunchback intent on surrendering a Jedi infant to the troops... a baby who turns out to be a fully grown, lightsaber-wielding Yoda.

Skywalker's choice to serve the Emperor and be renamed Darth Vader is not the only evolving relationship to be conferred here, either. While Yoda explains to Obi-Wan about communing with Qui-Gon Jinn in the film, the novel actually portrays one such discussion. Following his failure to best the Emperor in combat, Yoda converses with Jinn's disembodied voice and becomes aware of the potential to live on through the Force after death. In a parallel to young Skywalker's submission to the darkness, the elder Yoda pledges to open himself to new teachings and become Jinn's apprentice. Ironically, the Jedi uncover the means to avoid death, a talent that Sidious and Vader so desperately sought.

STAR WARS: REVENGE OF THE SITH | 89

Star Wars Episode III: Revenge Of The Sith

RELEASE DATE: May 5, 2005
PUBLISHER: Lucasarts

Unleashed on the public prior to the film's official premiere, the *Revenge of The Sith* videogame sees players battle through levels as either Anakin Skywalker or Obi-Wan Kenobi. The release stuck to the movie's plot and revolves around consequential moments, so supplementary themes do not truly materialize in this format.

However, the game spearheaded an appealing new approach to marketing a movie, previewing exclusive locales prior to their official arrival in cinemas, including the *Invisible Hand*, Utapau, and Mustafar. It also contained more than 10 minutes of actual scenes from the yet-to-be-released theatrical version. Such an extensive use of previously unseen footage is rarely seen outside of approved trailers and inexorably binds the game to its big-screen counterpart.

STAR WARS: REVENGE OF THE SITH SPECIAL

SITH UNSEEN

Dark Lord: The Rise of Darth Vader
(Legends)

AUTHOR: James Luceno
RELEASE DATE: November 22, 2005
PUBLISHER: Del Rey

The final entry in *The Dark Lord Trilogy*, *The Rise of Darth Vader* landed in stores several months after crowds first saw *Revenge of the Sith* in theaters, and James Luceno's novel catalogues the war's closing chapter, the Republic's transition into the Galactic Empire, and Darth Vader's early exploits as a Sith Lord.

Vader undertakes a mission to punish clone troopers who hesitated to carry out Order 66 on Murkhana, thus leading several Jedi to be spared the fate suffered by their peers. The Jedi struggle to deal with the confusion, presenting an eye-witness account from combatants far removed from the Council's inner circle during the war's abrupt end. The group react to factors outlined in the movie, including the Jedi Temple beacon's initial recall message, Kenobi's alternate order to hide, and a general puzzlement regarding what occurred between the Jedi and Palpatine.

Ultimately, only two Jedi escape the clutches of their pursuers and flee Murkhana. The elder one believes their cause to be lost and holds a desire to move on with his life, while his younger companion wishes to search for other survivors. The less experienced Jedi actually succeeds, assembling a rag-tag group who hope to stoke the Jedi Order's flame once

02

more. Their endeavor results in failure, as congregating together just makes it easier for Darth Sidious to trace their movements and wipe them all out at once. In this regard, the novel presents a logical reason why Yoda, Kenobi, and other Jedi stragglers select solitude instead of coordinating an effort to reform and initiate a counterattack against the Emperor.

The novel offers Darth Vader's reflections on his reimagined physical form in the weeks after his defeat on Mustafar. Vader internally expresses anger toward Palpatine and the medical droids who built his suit, as the ill-fitting armor hinders his movements, hampers his fighting technique, and causes him to feel imprisoned in its confines. The Sith Lord's dexterity gradually improves as he draws upon the dark side to engage and

slaughter several of the Jedi trying to consolidate their forces.

Another thread that extends from *Revenge of the Sith* pertains to Qui-Gon Jinn's reemergence and Luke Skywalker's concealment on Tatooine. Kenobi panics when he learns that Anakin lived, understandably concerned that placing the baby with the Lars family on the now-Lord Vader's homeworld puts Luke in danger. The novel reveals that Jinn reaches out to his former Padawan and assures him that Vader's fear of reliving painful memories prevents him from stepping foot on Tatooine. Author James Luceno connects Yoda's encouragement for Obi-Wan to commune with Qui-Gon with an explanation as to why Kenobi believes Luke will remain safe with the Lars on Tatooine.

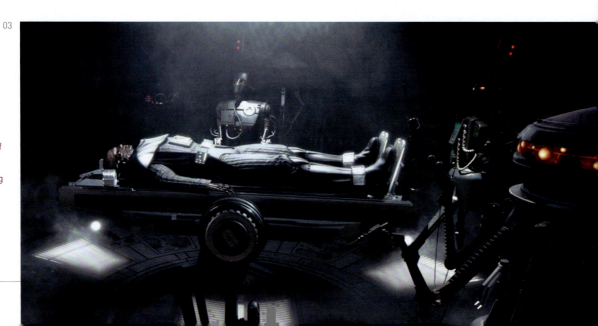

03

02 Beru (Bonnie Piesse) and Owen Lars (Joel Edgerton) were tasked with keeping Luke Skywalker safe on Tatooine at the end of *Revenge of the Sith*.

03 Anakin's terrifying transformation into Darth Vader was explored beyond the events of the movie in the novel *Dark Lord: The Rise of Darth Vader*.

THE SAGA CONTINUES

Despite all expectations, *Star Wars: Revenge of the Sith* turned out not to be the swansong of the Skywalker saga after all. In fact, George Lucas was already nurturing several ideas for new ventures across the galaxy far, far away before the movie was even released.

In July 2005, just a few short months after *Revenge of the Sith* debuted in theaters, Steve Sansweet, head of Fan Relations at Lucasfilm at that time, took to the stage at San Diego Comic-Con to update attending fans on the latest developments happening within Lucasfilm.

Following on from George Lucas' announcement of the forthcoming *The Clone Wars* animated series at *Star Wars* Celebration III in April, Sansweet had exciting news concerning the project being developed by the recently-formed Lucasfilm Animation division. Sansweet also announced that the recently formed Lucasfilm Animation division was busy developing a new project. "I'm very excited to be able to break the news," he told the expectant fans, "That pre-production has begun on the next generation of the *Star Wars* saga. A cutting edge, 30-minute 3D computer animation series based on the Clone Wars that takes place between Episode II and Episode III." The new series, which Sansweet described as a melding of Asian anime and unique 3D elements, was slated to start airing "sometime in 2007." In preparation, Lucasfilm had already hired a number of key production and creative talent to lead the development, including vice president and general manager Gail Currey, and executive producer Catherine Winder, as well as the head of Lucasfilm Animation in Singapore, Chris Kubsch.

Almost a year later, George Lucas was interviewed for MTV, where he discussed the future of Lucasfilm, a fourth Indiana Jones movie, and the much-anticipated animated *Star Wars* TV series. He confirmed that the series would take place during the Clone Wars and further chronicle the exploits and friendships of Jedi heroes Obi-Wan Kenobi and Anakin Skywalker while depicting epic battles set against a crumbling Republic. However, it would be a radical departure from Genndy Tartakovsky's *Clone Wars* micro-series, three short seasons of which had been released between *Attack of the Clones* and *Revenge of the Sith*. For starters, each episode would be much longer in duration, have more narrative depth, and eschew the stylized animation favored by Tartakovsky.

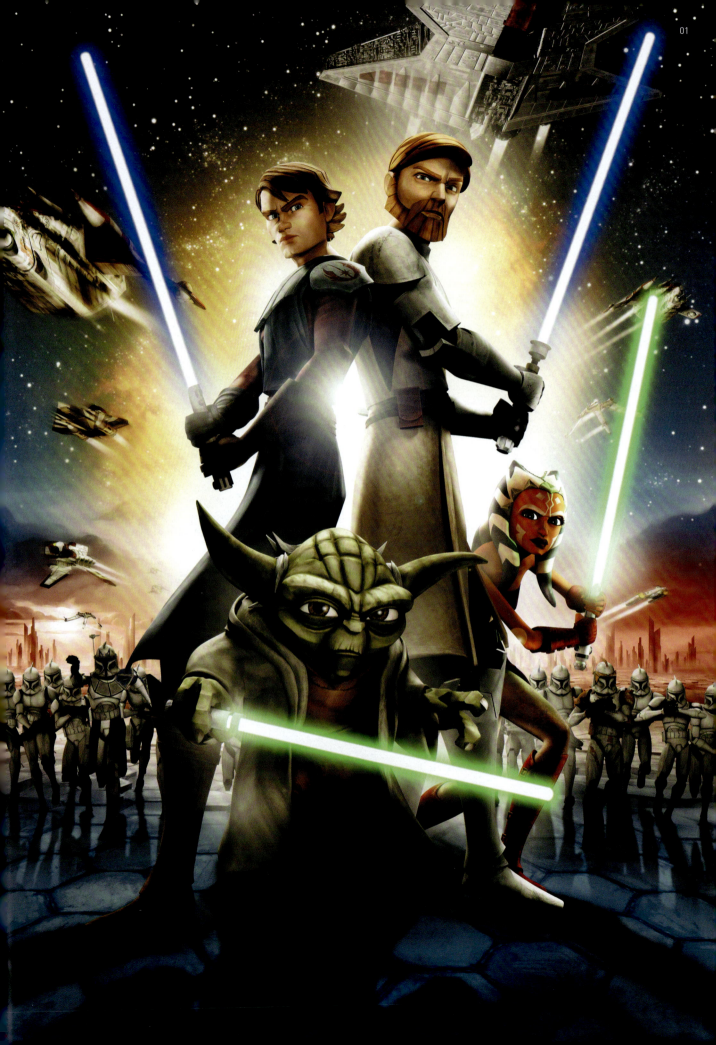

STAR WARS: REVENGE OF THE SITH SPECIAL
THE SAGA CONTINUES

"It's that same time period," Lucas said of what would become known as *Star Wars: The Clone Wars*. "But it's quite a bit more sophisticated, and it's not like anything you've ever seen on television before. [Tartakovsky] used his distinctive 2D style to do *Clone Wars*, but it was three minutes at a time, so it was a test subject. It worked and everything, but then we knew we were eventually going to do a 3D animated series."

Now scheduled to reach television screens in 2008, production was already well advanced. "We've got a number of episodes finished now," Lucas confirmed. "It looks really good. It's a lot of fun."

But Lucas had even grander plans, including a live-action *Star Wars* TV series that would bridge the gap between *Revenge of the Sith* and *A New Hope*, during what Obi-Wan Kenobi called the "dark times," with the Empire exerting its dominance over the galaxy, which he planned to begin work on following *The Clone Wars*' first season.

This series would shy away from the saga of the Skywalker family and instead focus on minor characters such as rebel and Imperial pilots. "None of the Skywalker story, none of that stuff is in there," Lucas explained. "It's completely different. The animated series has got all the characters in it, the one that comes after—the live-action one—is people who were in *Star Wars*, but they're not the main characters."

While the proposed live-action series would never see the light of day, *The Clone Wars* debuted with a feature-length episode that was released theatrically in 2008. The show ran for five seasons on Cartoon Network until 2013. A shorter, sixth season appeared on Netflix in 2014, and a seventh and final season was released on Disney+ in 2020, featuring storylines that dovetailed neatly with the events of *Revenge of the Sith* and the execution of Order 66.

During the MTV interview, Lucas looked back at the massive influence *Star Wars* had had on the popular culture of an entire generation. "It seems to have inspired a lot of people," he said. "But it's not just filmmakers. It's astronauts and people that go into business and people that do all kinds of things. *Star Wars* was really designed to make people think outside the box, to make people use their imagination and think anything is possible. And it does that."

03

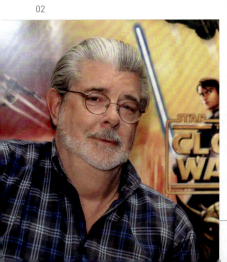

02

04

01 Previous page: Poster art promoting the theatrical release of *Star Wars: The Clone Wars*.

02 George Lucas explored the prequel era still further in *The Clone Wars*.

03 Count Dooku, voiced by Corey Burton.

04 Mace Windu (voiced by Terrence Carson) and Obi-Wan Kenobi (voiced by James Arnold Taylor).

05 Matt Lanter provided the voice of Anakin Skywalker in the series.

06 Ahsoka Tano (voiced by Ashley Eckstein) quickly became a fan-favorite character.

STAR WARS: REVENGE OF THE SITH | 95

MARVEL STUDIOS LIBRARY

MOVIE SPECIALS
- MARVEL STUDIOS' *SPIDER-MAN FAR FROM HOME*
- MARVEL STUDIOS' *ANT-MAN AND THE WASP*
- MARVEL STUDIOS' *AVENGERS: ENDGAME*
- MARVEL STUDIOS' *AVENGERS: INFINITY WAR*
- MARVEL STUDIOS' *BLACK PANTHER* (COMPANION)
- MARVEL STUDIOS' *BLACK WIDOW*
- MARVEL STUDIOS' *CAPTAIN MARVEL*
- MARVEL STUDIOS' THE FIRST TEN YEARS
- MARVEL STUDIOS' *THOR: RAGNAROK*
- MARVEL STUDIOS' *AVENGERS* AN INSIDER'S GUIDE TO THE *AVENGERS* FILMS
- MARVEL STUDIOS' *WANDAVISION*
- MARVEL STUDIOS' *THE FALCON AND THE WINTER SOLDIER*
- MARVEL STUDIOS' *LOKI*
- MARVEL STUDIOS' *ETERNALS*
- MARVEL STUDIOS' *HAWKEYE*
- MARVEL STUDIOS' *SPIDER-MAN: NO WAY HOME*

MARVEL STUDIOS' DOCTOR STRANGE IN THE MULTIVERSE OF MADNESS THE OFFICIAL MOVIE SPECIAL | MARVEL STUDIOS' PANTHER WAKANDA FOREVER THE OFFICIAL MOVIE SPECIAL | MARVEL STUDIOS' THOR: LOVE AND THUNDER THE OFFICIAL MOVIE SPECIAL | SPIDER-MAN ACROSS THE SPIDER-VERSE THE OFFICIAL MOVIE SPECIAL

MARVEL LEGACY LIBRARY

MARVEL'S *CAPTAIN AMERICA*: THE FIRST 80 YEARS | MARVEL'S *DAREDEVIL*: THE FIRST 60 YEARS | MARVEL'S *DEADPOOL*: THE FIRST 60 YEARS | MARVEL'S *FANTASTIC FOUR*: THE FIRST 60 YEARS | MARVEL'S *SPIDER-MAN*: THE FIRST 60 YEARS | MARVEL'S *WOLVERINE*: THE FIRST 50 YEARS | MARVEL'S *AVENGERS*: THE FIRST 60 YEARS

MARVEL CLASSIC NOVELS
- *WOLVERINE* WEAPON X OMNIBUS
- *SPIDER-MAN* THE DARKEST HOURS OMNIBUS
- *SPIDER-MAN* THE VENOM FACTOR OMNIBUS
- *X-MEN AND THE AVENGERS* GAMMA QUEST OMNIBUS
- *X-MEN* MUTANT EMPIRE OMNIBUS

NOVELS
- MARVEL'S GUARDIANS OF THE GALAXY NO GUTS, NO GLORY
- SPIDER-MAN MILES MORALES WINGS OF FURY
- MORBIUS THE LIVING VAMPIRE: BLOOD TIES
- ANT-MAN NATURAL ENEMY
- AVENGERS EVERYBODY WANTS TO RULE THE WORLD
- AVENGERS INFINITY
- BLACK PANTHER WHO IS THE BLACK PANTHER?

- CAPTAIN AMERICA DARK DESIGNS
- CAPTAIN MARVEL LIBERATION RUN
- CIVIL WAR
- DEADPOOL PAWS
- SPIDER-MAN YOUNG
- SPIDER-MAN KRAVEN'S LAST HUNT
- THANOS DEATH SENTENCE
- VENOM LETHAL PROTECTOR
- X-MEN DAYS OF FUTURE PAST
- X-MEN THE DARK PHOENIX SAGA
- SPIDER-MAN HOSTILE TAKEOVER
- BLACK PANTHER: TALES OF WAKANDA
- BLACK PANTHER: PANTHER'S RAGE
- MARVEL'S ORIGINAL SIN
- MARVEL'S MIDNIGHT SUNS: INFERNAL RISING
- GUARDIANS OF THE GALAXY – ANNIHILATION: CONQUEST
- MARVEL'S SECRET INVASION
- CAPTAIN MARVEL: SHADOW CODE
- LOKI: JOURNEY INTO MYSTERY
- DOCTOR STRANGE: DIMENSION WAR

ART BOOKS
- MARVEL'S *GUARDIANS OF THE GALAXY*: THE ART OF THE GAME
- MARVEL'S *AVENGERS: BLACK PANTHER*: WAR FOR WAKANDA EXPANSION: ART OF THE HIDDEN KINGDOM
- MARVEL'S *SPIDER-MAN: MILES MORALES* – THE ART OF THE GAME
- MARVEL STUDIOS' THE INFINITY SAGA – *THE AVENGERS*: THE ART OF THE MOVIE
- MARVEL'S *SPIDER-MAN* THE ART OF THE GAME
- MARVEL *CONTEST OF CHAMPIONS* THE ART OF THE BATTLEREALM
- *SPIDER-MAN: INTO THE SPIDER-VERSE* THE ART OF THE MOVIE
- MARVEL STUDIOS' THE INFINITY SAGA – *IRON MAN*: THE ART OF THE MOVIE
- MARVEL STUDIOS' THE INFINITY SAGA – *IRON MAN 2*: THE ART OF THE MOVIE
- MARVEL STUDIOS' THE INFINITY SAGA – *IRON MAN 3*: THE ART OF THE MOVIE
- MARVEL STUDIOS' THE INFINITY SAGA – *CAPTAIN AMERICA: THE WINTER SOLDIER*: THE ART OF THE MOVIE
- MARVEL STUDIOS' THE INFINITY SAGA – *THOR*: THE ART OF THE MOVIE
- MARVEL STUDIOS' THE INFINITY SAGA – *THOR: THE DARK WORLD*: THE ART OF THE MOVIE
- MARVEL STUDIOS' THE INFINITY SAGA – *CAPTAIN AMERICA: THE FIRST AVENGER*: THE ART OF THE MOVIE

STAR WARS LIBRARY

   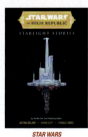 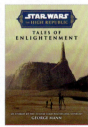  

STAR WARS: THE MANDALORIAN GUIDE TO SEASON ONE | STAR WARS: THE MANDALORIAN GUIDE TO SEASON TWO | STAR WARS INSIDER PRESENTS THE DARK SIDE COLLECTION | STAR WARS THE HIGH REPUBLIC STARLIGHT STORIES | STAR WARS THE HIGH REPUBLIC TALES OF ENLIGHTENMENT | STAR WARS: THE RETURN OF THE JEDI 40TH ANNIVERSARY SPECIAL | STAR WARS: THE PHANTOM MENACE 25TH ANNIVERSARY SPECIAL

- *ROGUE ONE: A STAR WARS STORY* THE OFFICIAL COLLECTOR'S EDITION
- *ROGUE ONE: A STAR WARS STORY* THE OFFICIAL MISSION DEBRIEF
- *STAR WARS: THE LAST JEDI* THE OFFICIAL COLLECTOR'S EDITION
- *STAR WARS: THE LAST JEDI* THE OFFICIAL MOVIE COMPANION
- *STAR WARS: THE LAST JEDI* THE ULTIMATE GUIDE
- *SOLO: A STAR WARS STORY* THE OFFICIAL COLLECTOR'S EDITION
- *SOLO: A STAR WARS STORY* THE ULTIMATE GUIDE
- *THE BEST OF STAR WARS INSIDER* VOLUME 1
- *THE BEST OF STAR WARS INSIDER* VOLUME 2
- *THE BEST OF STAR WARS INSIDER* VOLUME 3

- *THE BEST OF STAR WARS INSIDER* VOLUME 4
- *STAR WARS:* LORDS OF THE SITH
- *STAR WARS:* HEROES OF THE FORCE
- *STAR WARS:* ICONS OF THE GALAXY
- *STAR WARS:* THE SAGA BEGINS
- *STAR WARS* THE ORIGINAL TRILOGY
- *STAR WARS:* ROGUES, SCOUNDRELS AND BOUNTY HUNTERS
- *STAR WARS:* CREATURES, ALIENS, AND DROIDS
- *STAR WARS: THE RISE OF SKYWALKER* THE OFFICIAL COLLECTOR'S EDITION

- *STAR WARS: THE MANDALORIAN:* GUIDE TO SEASON ONE
- *STAR WARS: THE MANDALORIAN:* GUIDE TO SEASON TWO
- *STAR WARS: THE EMPIRE STRIKES BACK* THE 40TH ANNIVERSARY SPECIAL EDITION
- *STAR WARS: AGE OF RESISTANCE* THE OFFICIAL COLLECTOR'S EDITION
- *STAR WARS: THE SKYWALKER SAGA* THE OFFICIAL COLLECTOR'S EDITION
- *STAR WARS INSIDER:* FICTION COLLECTION VOLUME 1
- *STAR WARS INSIDER:* FICTION COLLECTION VOLUME 2
- *STAR WARS INSIDER PRESENTS: MANDALORIAN SEASON 2* VOLUME 1
- *STAR WARS INSIDER PRESENTS: MANDALORIAN SEASON 2* VOLUME 2

AVAILABLE AT ALL GOOD BOOKSTORES AND ONLINE

titan-comics.com | titanbooks.com

© 2024 Lucasfilm Ltd. and ™. All Rights Reserved. Used Under Authorization.
© 2025 MARVEL

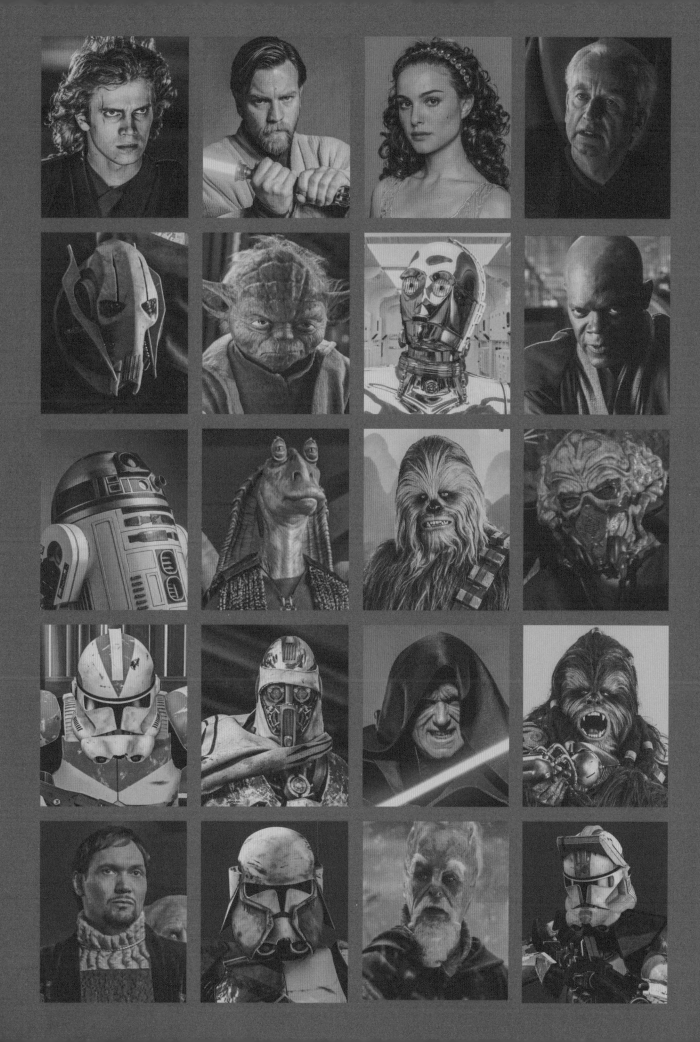